FOREWORD

For years now, I have been helping businesses learn how to improve their Google presence in ways that comply with Google's Guidelines. I am completely obsessed with understanding Google's algorithm changes, but most people don't nerd out on penalties, audits, and algorithms like I do.

I believe that having a foundational understanding of how people are engaging and experiencing search is critical to the success of our businesses. You don't have to understand or master the technical logic behind Google's algorithms. However, you should understand the trends of consumer behavior as millions of people begin their discovery and research process through an online or voice search.

Discovered gives you an understanding of why so many brands struggle to gain traction and momentum online. This book takes a holistic look at the connected customer experience, consumer psychology, and common mistakes that prevent Marketing Leaders from reaching their goals. Discovered curates hard to find data with emerging technologies, to give you real-world examples to apply to any brand's Digital Marketing strategies.

As Marketers, we often compete in a busy online marketplace where our brand gets lost in a sea of ads, videos, and content. As our ad spend is increases, our reach and returns decrease. Discovered also provides an in-depth look at the Voice market and how people are discovering, engaging, and connecting with new brands daily. This book is the handbook for brands that are looking for a way innovate using voice and helps you get started with voice.

Yesterday's thinking is today's baggage, and organizations that want to lead and shape their industry must evolve and adapt with technology and innovative thinking. Read about how brands have created innovative experiences leveraging emerging technology to elevate the customer's online experience with their brand.

Create a purposeful, delightful, and memorable customer experience so that people share it. Give your online content meaning and context, so the search engines understand it. Once the search engines understand and trust your brands content, you are ready to begin your voice journey. A voice journey that will add value your shoppers lives every step of the way. Google, your brand, and your shoppers want you to provide the best possible customer experiences. Discovered will give you the knowledge you desire to create unforgettable and transformational customer search experiences.

Dr. Marie Haynes
MarieHaynes.com

TABLE OF CONTENTS

DISCOVERED

Dominate online and voice search without wasting time or money

BETHANIE NONAMI

DISCOVERED

This is the first edition. If you'd like to make suggestions for a future edition, please email hello@discoveredbook.com. We appreciate you.

For permission requests, speaking, inquiries and bulk order options, email hello@discoveredbook.com.

Library of Congress Cataloging-in-Publication Data in progress

Paperback ISBN: 978-0-578-54164-8

Printed in the United States

INTRODUCTION

I love what I do. I started programming when I was in elementary school – back when a computer was just a big dusty dirt-gray-colored box with a green screen and a keyboard. This was before Windows was a thing, and the mouse didn't even exist.

I am one of those nerdy people who gets excited about every new technology, especially if the technology changes the way we experience life. In my lifetime, I have witnessed three major waves of life-changing technology: Windows, the Internet, and smartphones. Even if you aren't a huge fan of technology in general or new applications in particular, you may be hustling for your amazing brand to be discovered by more people. You might spend a lot of time and money on all the things brands are supposed to do:

- Social media strategies
- Digital strategies
- Paid ad strategies
- And the list goes on and on.

You know these are the things that you "should do" according to countless agencies, experts, and high-paid consultants. But you feel, no, you know, that this can't be all there is. You know there has to be a better way.

There *is* a better way, but that path is the one that is often less traveled. One may consider it unchartered territory.

- Yes, it involves more risk than you may be used to.
- No, it may not have been done before.

- No, we don't know what your exact return on investment or efforts may be.
- Yes, I definitely recommend following this path!

If you made decisions solely on ROI, you probably wouldn't be executing half of the strategies you do right now anyway. Right?

We are reaching this perfect moment in time where the time to ideate, design, test, and launch new technology is the fastest it has ever been in history. New technologies are released every day.

Martech is technology that focuses on marketing software, technology, or automation. According to ChiefMartech.com, Martech exceeded 7,040 different solutions. This category of software solutions has nearly tripled, since 2015. Over 7,000 solutions today are solely designed just to help you improve marketing. No wonder you have so many strategies and shiny object tactics!

Ryan Deiss of Digital Marketer explains our marketing efforts as broken bridges. You are trying to cross a valley to get to a magnificent mountain, we'll call it the Motherland. The Motherland represents your biggest marketing goals and dreams. The only way to the Motherland is to build a bridge from where you stand today over the valley to the Motherland. You start building your bridges and you start with a website bridge. As you are halfway through your website bridge, someone tells you there is a faster bridge you can build to get to the Motherland. This new bridge is called the social media bridge. You stop building the website bridge and start building your social media bridge. The social media bridge doesn't get you across the valley as fast as you hoped, so you hire some workers to finish the social media bridge. You take a step back and look at the majestic mountain on the other side of the valley. You decide go back through your "World's Greatest Marketing Bridge" research and decide to build an Influencer bridge. Since setting your eyes on the Marketing Motherland, years have passed. Without evening realizing you have built a valley of broken bridges.

More than 7,000 different marketing technology software applications shows us there are thousands of potential bridges we can build. But just because we can, it doesn't mean we should. Part of our jobs as leaders are to know where to focus and when to pivot.

> *"The only limit to our realization of tomorrow will be our doubts of today."*
>
> -Franklin Roosevelt

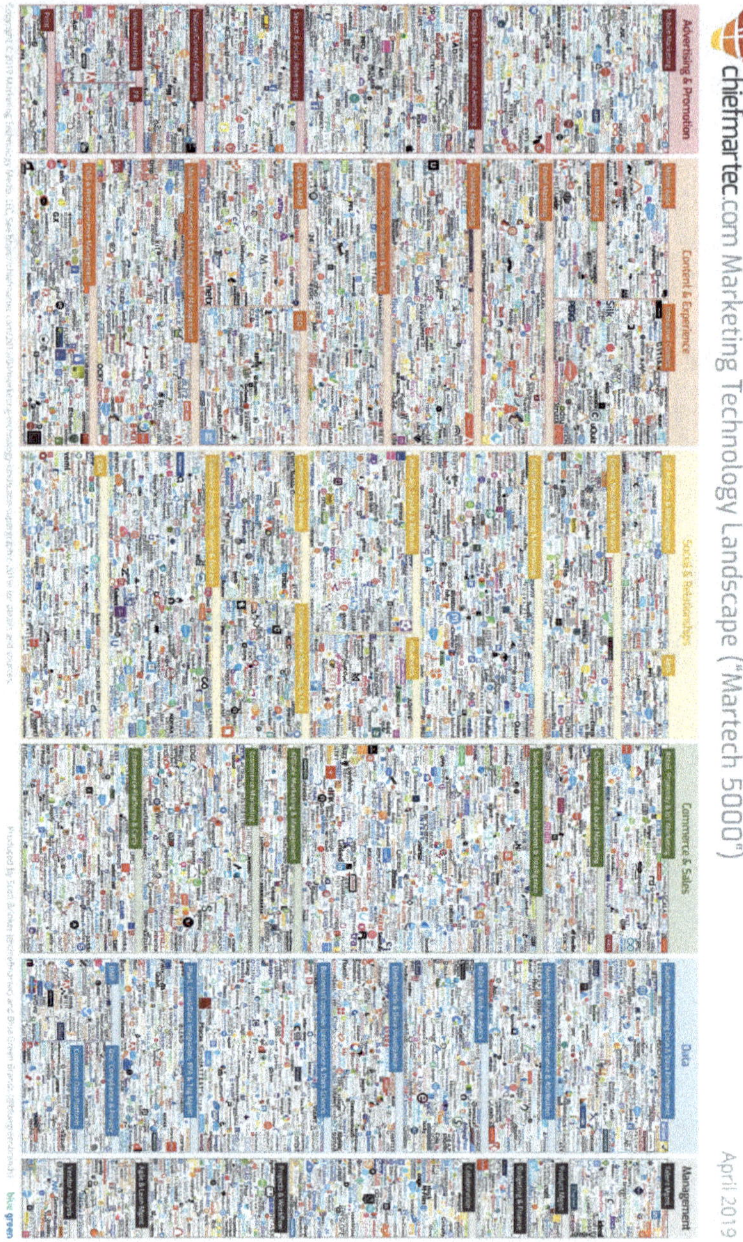

Source: ChiefMartec.com Image[1]

Say OK Google - Talk to Discovered Book – Martech Image

ChiefMartech.com knows that this graphic is a bit hard to read, so they have made a list of the vendors available in a Google Sheets too[2]!

If you have thousands of options and even more opinions, what do you do? You innovate! You adapt faster than your competition. You do something no one else has the guts to do. This means you are the person heading off to sea when everyone thinks the world is flat. Sounds scary? You bet. Are people going to call you crazy? Maybe. Sounds super exciting? Absolutely!

By reading this book, you will gain an understanding of how to leverage the power of emerging technology and innovation to forge a new path. A path that will be nearly impossible for your competitors to mimic. A path that will help your brand have such an unfair advantage, it almost feels like cheating. But it definitely feels good when you can lead and shape your industry.

This book focuses on what the next big wave of changes that are already here but are often unknown and underutilized to brand leaders. These technologies and innovations span Online Search, Voice, Voice Search, Voice Assistants, Intelligent Assistants (or bots), and world of conversational and community engagement. By the end of this book you will understand how you can use these technologies to begin or continue your brand's innovation journey by future-proofing your brand's position in your industry.

---

[2] *Say OK Google - Talk to Discovered Book – Martech Companies*

Future-Proof

Adjective (of a product) unlikely to become obsolete

Verb make (a product or system) future-proof

Many companies think they are innovating. It may be a pillar of success or a core value. However, many aren't actually innovating, they are just iterating. There's a difference. They may be trying to improve an existing process, ad campaign, or community to make it better. Iteration and optimization are important processes but they are not innovation. This is what most companies are really doing, trying to get better results. But this is not innovation.

How can brands survive in a world with:

- Less attention from consumers,
- Emerging startups popping up on every street corner,
- Juggling the consumer's massive desire and expectation for personalization,
- More data than our tiny human brains can process?

Search and Innovate. Innovate and Search.

The best chance we have is to innovate. The first place you need to start with innovation is where 84% of people start the customer journey, with a search[3]. 90% of shoppers use search across the entire buying journey[4].

Even if innovation seems too risky or radical for your organization, you owe it to yourself, professionally, to read this book and understand not only what is coming but what is already here today.

People are tired of scrolling through page 1 of Google searching for an answer. They want THE right answer now. Put yourself in their shoes. How much time do you want to look for an answer to a question? How many times do you want to click on a link, skim the page for the answer, and click back to look for another page with a better answer? My guess is you said less than three. Nobody wants to hunt for answers.

Consumer shopping behavior changes so rapidly because people are trying to get to the right answer faster. We have become distracted, impatient, and lazy. Consumers demand THE right answer. Search engines are becoming answer engines. Search queries have evolved from keywords to questions spoken in a conversational manner. Smart speakers, voice-activated searches, and voice assistant platforms are providing 1-3 top answers, not 15 of them, like Page 1. Depending on the voice platform, there may be just one answer.

In 2018, there were 250 billion searches made through voice[5]. In Voicebot.ai's Voice Assistant SEO Report for Brands, out of 200 leading brands analyzed:

- 26.5% have some sort of voice app for Alexa,
- 21.5% have one for Google Assistant,
- And about 15% have a presence on both platforms.

---

[3] *Say OK Google - Talk to Discovered Book - Deloitte Search*
[4] *Say OK Google - Talk to Discovered Book - Forrester Search*
[5] *Say OK Google - Talk to Discovered Book - Voicebot SEO Report*

Is your brand in question or are you the answer? If you don't believe me, just ask Alexa, Siri, or OK Google a question.

What are the questions that consumers ask to discover your brand? You can try questions with and without your brand name, like these:

- What is non-dairy ice cream made from?
- What healthy snacks can toddlers eat?
- What does non-GMO mean?
- Is organic food really better than non-organic foods?

Think of a couple of questions and ask your smartphone voice assistant (Siri, Bixby, Google Assistant) or Alexa or Google Home. What did she say?

If she couldn't answer the question, then you are looking at a new channel filled with opportunity!

This is a super exciting time for future-focused brands that are willing to use innovation to learn better ways to connect to shoppers.

Brands can't afford to take a wait-and-see posture when it comes to adapting and evolving as our shoppers are every day. If you are ready to learn ways to leverage emerging technology and innovation so your brand can be discovered by more of the right people, then let's do this!

High fives and fist bumps,

Bethanie Nonami

P.S.

This book is based on my 28-plus years of experience to give you an accelerated way to learn quickly so you can begin to innovate. It is by no means meant to exclude a particular vendor, software, or methodology. Since technology changes rapidly, it would be impossible to always have the latest and greatest in the book, but never fear, you can visit Discoveredbook.com/ Book to find the latest and greatest of what we love, use, and recommend.

P.P.S.

If you enjoy this book, find it useful, or take action, I would love to know about it. I read it all and I would love to know what you liked and what I could have been done better. To leave a review, please visit DiscoveredBook.com/ Reviews. If you have feedback or recommendations to make the book more useful or incredible resources that you have found that helped you, please share them with me. You can reach me directly at Bethanie@DiscoveredBook.com or on Twitter or LinkedIn @BethanieNonami.

P.P.P.S.

Bullies suck. Cyberbullies suck more. I have children, who have and will probably continue to Google me and read everything they find. Are all kids nosey, or just mine? I respect your opinion and I respect your voice but if you have harsh words for me, please respect the power of the Internet and the damage it can do. I am not perfect and I want to hear your opinion, especially if it can help me grow, be a better person, or understand a point of view that I don't understand now. But I am also a stubborn, head-strong Aries, who loves a great debate. All that I ask is that you bring it privately. Please email me at Bethanie@DiscoveredBook.com.

Please be kind to others.

The world would be a better place if we treated each other with kindness.

HOW TO USE THIS BOOK

1. This icon means you can speak the command into Google Assistant. Just ask your Google Assistant to "*Talk to Discovered Book*" and then say the phrase next to the icon. Viola. Voice magic!
2. Images appear small in print, to see the full image, speak the voice command into Google Assistant or visit DiscoveredBook.com for a larger image. Just look for the Chapter name and footnote # to find the image. Poof! Web magic!

DEDICATION

This book is dedicated to my husband, Damion. Without your love, support, and shift kicks, I wouldn't be the woman I am today. You catch me when I fall and have always been my rock. Thank you for continuing to love my Flaws and All. I love you more than I can ever fully express.

To Dame, Eliana, and Ashley, you are the reasons I do what I do. I am so grateful for you every day. You are what fuels my fire and ignites my drive. You make me proud every day. I love you more.

PREFACE

> *"Insanity is doing the same thing over and over again and expecting different results."*
>
> – Albert Einstein

Isn't that what most of us do on a daily basis? If you're in a leadership role, your work may be measured by sales. Tactics that worked three years, or even one year ago, don't yield the same results as they did before. Most of us are seeing our ad costs increase, our reach decrease, and are continually challenged with making our marketing dollars stretch further than ever before.

Executing against the same strategies as last quarter and running the same campaigns won't cut it. Perhaps you're making minor tweaks to the last initiative but aren't you just doing different iterations of the same thing?

I'm not implying that you're insane but there is a better way.

We live in a technologically advanced time. We have access to more data than any other time in history, which is awesome *if* that data provides valuable insights. "I just want one more report!" said no one ever. We need actionable insights in order to connect with our shoppers better. Ideally, we want to turn that insight into increasing value, brand affinity, and sales.

It is important to understand how to leverage proven emerging technologies to future-proof both your brand's online and voice presence. As human beings, we are always evolving. The brands that deserve to win should be shaping, influencing, and leading shopper behavior instead of scrambling to one-up the competition or trying to keep up with old behaviors.

You may already employ these marketing strategies:

- AdWords or paid media
- Social media campaigns
- Influencer tactics
- Brand awareness

That's a start, but these strategies alone are not enough.

You have to go beyond strategy to determine where the puck is going, not where it has been.

I'm not a big hockey fan but I have mad respect Wayne Gretzky. Like Gretzky, I've made a career out of understanding where the puck is going, not where it has been.

Many of us spend our days trying to figure out how can we just move the needle a teeny-tiny-itsy bit. We spend our days trying to solve problems.

- How can we increase this conversion by 1%?
- How can we increase our engagement with our consumers?
- How can we increase our reach or brand awareness with people that are searching for a product?

These may seem like problems but they aren't problems, they're only inhibitors.

Inhibitors -Things that are preventing your success. They pop-up like moles in the Whack-A-Mole game. Once you hit one mole, another one pops up. They are expected.

Problems - These are overarching pillars in your business. If you focused on improving one pillar, you would knock out multiple moles at once.

Here is an example of inhibitors a brand may face:

- Lack of consumer awareness
- Lack of brand recognition
- Lack of market share
- Low website conversions
- Very little engagement online channels
- No demand from retailers
- No demand from the public
- Long sales cycles - too much education

Here are some of the bigger problems the brand may have:

- Lack of Clarity
- Lack of Credibility
- Lack of Connectivity
- Lack of Visibility

Let's take clarity as an example. If you choose to focus on just one area and you improved that by 10%, what problems could that solve for the brand?

Improving Clarity may solve these inhibitors:

- Product market fit
- Brand differentiators
- Brand message
- Brand voice
- Target market

You can see how improving one of the core problems could easily knock out several inhibitors.

What are the real problems in your business that would eliminate or greatly reduce your inhibitors if you gave them a little more time and attention?

Understanding the difference between inhibitors and problems has been game-changing for my business and our clients. I learned this notion from my business mentor, Topher Morrison, one of the most brilliant people I know[6]. You can also read more about it in the book "Become a Key Person of Influence: The Five-Step Sequence to Becoming One of the Most Highly Valued and Highly Paid People in Your Industry" by Daniel Priestley[7] with Foreword by Topher Morrison.

One of the things I constantly hear is, "Consumers' behaviors are rapidly changing. It evolves so quickly and we can't even keep up with it. They're just avoiding our ads and we don't know how to respond."

Yes, their behavior is changing quickly. But guess what? So is yours.

Let's look at your own search or buying behavior. How you behaved six months ago is probably different than how you search today. There are things that have served us

---

[6] *Say OK Google - Talk to Discovered Book - Topher Morrison*

[7] *Say OK Google - Talk to Discovered Book - KPI*

well in the past such as avatars, demographics, and personas but the buying journey has become more complex. The journey is not linear. It's hundreds of touchpoints interwoven like an intricate spider's web.

> Shoppers have become a **highly personalized marketplace of one**. Your brand is serving millions of single shopper marketplaces

Shoppers know we are tracking data on what they like, how they shop, and their personal preferences. The brands that deliver highly customized experiences have elevated the experiential expectation of our shoppers for all of us.

As a brand you can combine today's consumer behavior with your intimate knowledge of your shopper and technology to create incredible shopper experiences.

Here are a couple of trends we've seen:

- 84% of transactions start with a search[3].
- 90% of people use search across the entire buying journey[4].
- Voice is estimated to be valued at $80 billion by 2023[8].

---

[8] *Say OK Google - Talk to Discovered Book – $80 Billion*

- 1 billion Google Voice Assistants are active today[9].
- 3.25 billion voice activated devices are in use today and may reach 8 billion by 2023[8].
- $17 million was lost in 2019 due to lack of visibility on voice search[10].
- Highly personalized, unique experiences are expected and almost demanded.
- Voice is not coming, it's mass and it's here.
- Artificial intelligence, machine learning, and deep learning all help us make better decisions to create better buying journeys.

This book will tell you about ways to leverage voice and search to give your brand an understanding of how you could be competing in order to lead the pack, not follow it.

The bar has been set even higher than it's ever been before, which is making our jobs harder.

Brands that are future-focused will be the ones that stand out and win in this personalized shopper experiential world. This is not something that any brand, regardless of target market, can afford to wait any longer to think about.

Golden opportunities

When your go-to voice assistants can't answer a question, it's because they don't know the answer. This is the first time in more than 20 years that a brand can enter into a channel with such a low barrier of entry.

---

[9] *Say OK Google - Talk to Discovered Book– 1 Billion Google Assistants*

[10] *Say OK Google - Talk to Discovered Book - $17M Lost*

Unless brands are aware of what is going on with voice search, they risk not being found and relying on third parties to answer consumer questions about *their brand*. In Voicebot.ai's Voice Assistant SEO Report for Brands, the results of an extensive study show that branded and category queries often result in an error or no response on Alexa, Apple, and Samsung. Google is leading the way with the correct information on voice searches[11].

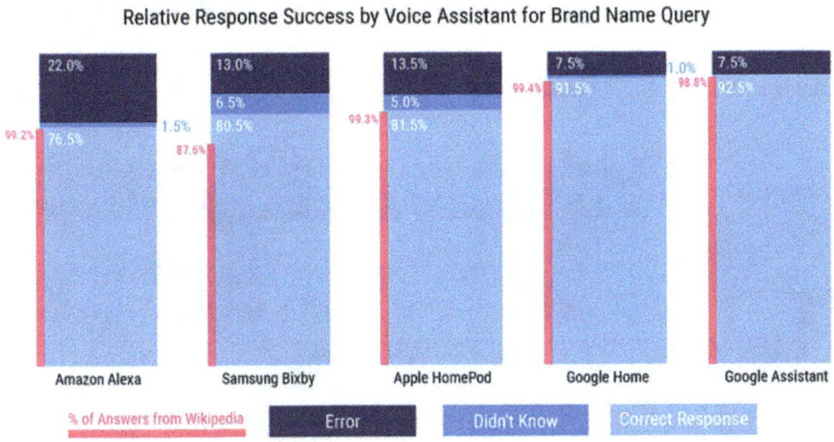

Source: Voicebot.ai Voice Assistant SEO Report for Brands[11]
Say OK Google - Talk to Discovered Book – Voice Responses

In many cases, when there is an answer, it is often provided by a third party, not by the brand. Since each voice assistant platform has its own process to find answers, the voice search engines often don't turn to brand pages for the answer. 5 of the 5 voice platforms are relying heavily on Wikipedia as a source of voice answers[12]. If your brand has a Wiki page, the first 29 words

[11] *Say OK Google - Talk to Discovered Book – Voice Responses*

[12] *Say OK Google - Talk to Discovered Book – Third Party Responses*

could be what your shoppers are hearing when they ask question about your brand on voice.

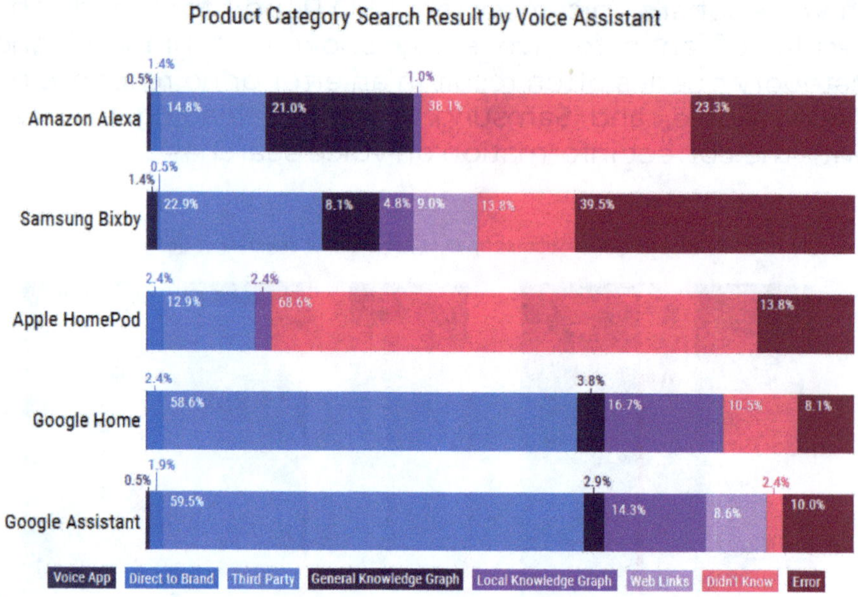

Source: Voicebot.ai Voice Assistant SEO Report for Brands[12]
Say OK Google - Talk to Discovered Book – Third Party Responses

An overwhelming percentage of the responses are from third parties (Google, WiKi, or Yelp). Or the voice assistant doesn't know the answers and errors (on every other platform). This means that your brand probably doesn't control the answer to questions **about your brand.**

When shoppers ask voice where to purchase, the results may surprise you. On all 5 voice platforms, the brand is used less than 10% of the time. On Google, the Local Knowledge Graph (Google My Business, Google Shopping connected to geo and inventory) is leading the pack. 80%-100% of the time on Alexa, Samsung, and Apple results in no response or an error. This is worth repeated and rereading. 80%-100% of the time on any platform other than Google, voice platforms do not know where to tell shoppers to purchase your products. Your only chance of survival on Google is on Google owned channels.

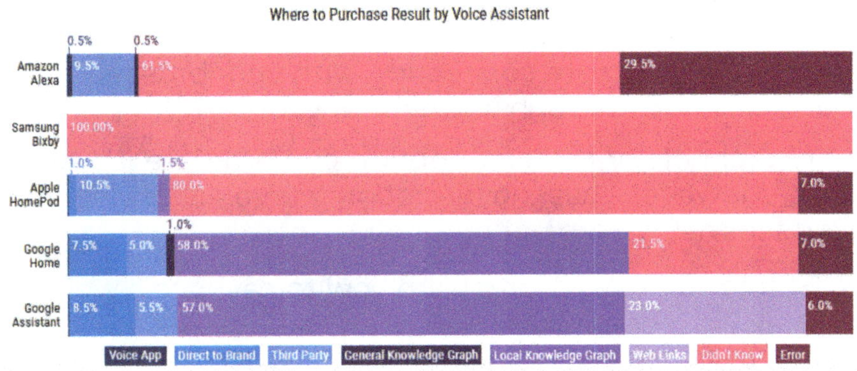

Source: Voicebot.ai Voice Assistant SEO Report for Brands[13]

Say OK Google - Talk to Discovered Book – Shopping Responses

Your brand must optimize your brand's presence for voice on your **branded channels** AND on **Google channels, Wiki, and Yelp** ASAP!

Voice is a first-generation search and shopping channel and it is not yet over-saturated; rather, it is still being defined and discovered. The time, effort, risk, and cost to enter the voice channel is relatively low compared to other channels.

This is like 1998 when SEO was just starting to become a thing. Even though SEO had already been around for years, bloggers and companies thought, "I'm just going to have my website up. That's enough for it to take off. I'm going to wait and see what this SEO jazz is all about before wasting time on it." Everyone thought it was just a fad. No, it was a REALLY big deal.

What's interesting is that voice allows people to engage and interact with the brand on a whole new level. You can now have an intimate connection with your prospects and your customers through a conversation.

Every technology has an adoption curve before it's mass. Voice, however, has no adoption curve. It is the first interface that we are not required to learn.

- Internet - We had to learn how to navigate a website, make unintuitive pages, and make sense of it all.
- Search - We had to learn how to ask stupid questions. We had to speak like a caveman and say "dry cleaners" or "elementary school."
- Smartphones - We had to learn how to swipe or tap, not double click.

Voice, on the other hand, is being adopted at a faster pace than previous technologies, including the Internet and smartphones **combined**.

This is a massive opportunity for brands to not only create a deeper connection with their consumers but to learn from actual shopper conversations about the connection people want to have with your brand.

With more than 3.25 billion active voice-assisted devices (between smartphones and smart speakers) in use today and an estimated 8 billion by 2023[8], brands can't afford to wait and see any longer.

A recent Adobe survey found that 91% of business decision makers invest in voice today and voice commerce is the top objective of nearly half of them[14].

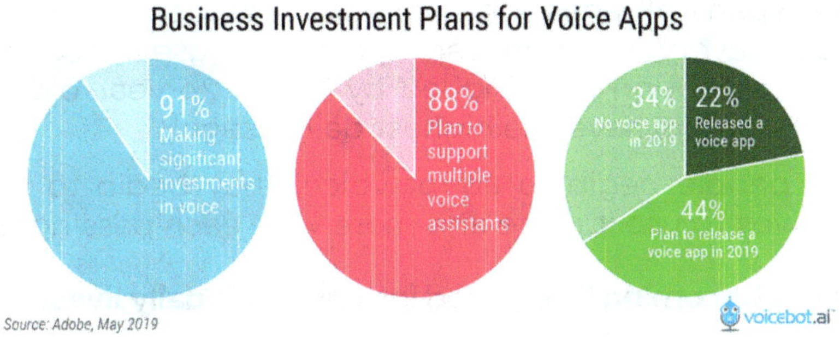

Source: Voicebot.ai, Adobe Insights[14]

Say OK Google - Talk to Discovered Book - Business Investments in Voice

Voice is a new behavior

Voice isn't a replacement behavior, it is a new behavior that people are adding to their lives. Have you ever heard the saying, "What did we do with our time before Facebook, smartphones, Netflix, etc.?" View voice through the same lens. Voice is a behavior that people are doing in addition to their old behaviors.

Voice doesn't replace SEO (search engine optimization or how you are found online in search) and voice won't eliminate other platforms or channels like social media. Voice is a complementary channel to what is already happening.

> When thinking about voice,
> you should think **voice AND**....

Voice spans all ages, demographics, and socioeconomic groups. Everyone who can speak can use voice. Even though adoption is being led by 18- to 24-year-olds, the Baby Boomers have the highest daily usage[15].

Once people begin to adopt voice, they begin to adapt their lives to use it more and more with each passing day.

Voice is becoming integrated into people's daily lives.[15]

Once people use voice, their behavior changes

- 89% use them it daily
- 33% use voiceover 5 times a day
- 28% use voice 4-5 times a day
- 24% use voice 2-3 times a day

Voice is not only a channel, it's an enabler. It is rapidly becoming an enabler of online, interactive, hands-free shopping. You can buy without ever having to click a single link or visit a website at all. Consumers can shop on voice across seven different device platforms completely hands-free.

Voice provides the opportunity for brands to play a more intimate role in the daily lives of your shoppers and your existing customers. You have a chance to become a part of their shopping routines and habits or you have a chance to be useful and build brand affinity during the research and discovery phase all the way through the purchase and beyond.

Companies have the opportunity to not only create a stronger bond and connection with people but own the conversation and own the voice and persona of their brand. Voice allows you to have a direct-to-consumer conversation and relationship. Voice is the most humanly

---

[15] *Say OK Google - Talk to Discovered Book –Daily Voice Habits*

connected channel we have. It is how we create bonds, trust, and nurture relationships...with communication and language.

Consumers are also beginning to understand how voice technology can make their lives easier. They can discover new brands, whether shopping at home on smart speakers or when doing cardio in the gym or in the carpool pick-up line at school.

The interaction that consumers expect to have with their brands is extremely, almost unbelievably, personalized. People don't mind ads as much if they are valuable and personalized.

Shoppers welcome ads that are **personalized and customized.**

Brands that invest the time in understanding your shoppers will discover their preferences when it comes to:

- Buying
- Diet (food, allergies, restrictions)
- Lifestyle
- Content
- Platforms
- Communication (email, text, chat, phone)
- Engagement
- Community
- Advertisements

- And much more

This empowers you to give shoppers a remarkable experience that feels customized just for them.

As mentioned, this also gives brands the ability to create a meaningful direct-to-consumer channel. If yours is a larger brand, you may be stuck in the middle of a world of retailer rules and restrictions. You have to play by the retailer rules to appear on shelf, only to compete with private label products and challenger brands in store. You may or may not have control over your retailer item pages, product category listings, or ads on retailer-specific platforms. **It's the song you have to dance to and sometimes you hate the music.**

Voice gives you a way to focus on a brand-owned channel that **you control.** You can give the shopper an option of how and where they want to buy or you can steer the path to a preferred eCommerce channel or retailer. Either way, voice may give your brand a new way to:

- Create an incredible experience
- Own the conversation
- Build the paths, journeys, and conversations
- Validate your assumptions
- Collect specific-shopper conversational insights
- Collect shopper phone numbers or emails
- Retarget or market to shoppers organically
- Create and nurture a community
- Control where to send retailer sales
- Create a brand persona with an authentic voice

Although voice is a fairly new channel, people are actively making purchases today and more people are considering making future purchases on voice.

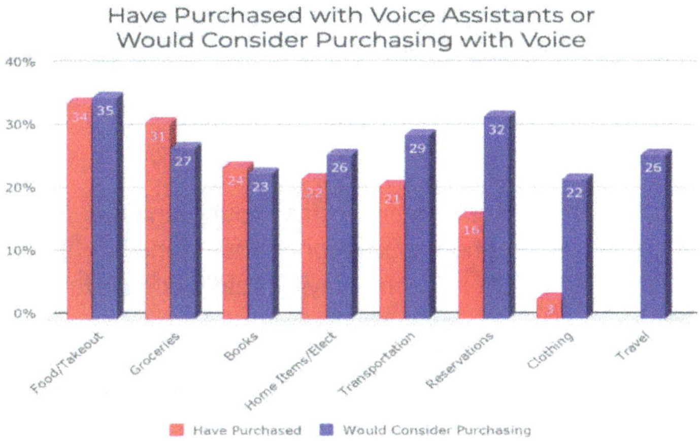

Source: PwC, Prepare for the Voice Revolution[16]
Say OK Google - Talk to Discovered Book - Purchased on Voice

According to the Grocery Manufacturers Association with PWC, at least 40% of consumer brands sell direct to customers in some manner[17]. Many brands are trying to figure out how to grow this business as rapidly as possible.

There is immense value in having a direct to consumer channel that you can create and own the shopper conversation.

Source: PwC Global Insights, It's time for a consumer-centered metric: introducing 'Return on Experience.'[18]
Say OK Google - Talk to Discovered Book - Return on Experience

---

[17] *Say OK Google - Talk to Discovered Book - Direct to consumers*

No matter how big or small your brand is, no matter how much money your brand has to spend, right now, **the playing field is completely level for all brands.**

Nike, for instance, has been very clear that they intend to grow their direct-to-consumer business and that has been the focus. Nike announced they want to grow their channel by 250% to a $16 billion market in the next five years. In 2016, nearly a quarter of Nike's total sales were generated through such channels[19].

This is not only a focus for well-established brands, but also startups are making a deliberate choice to avoid retailers altogether. In fact, some startups are building their product roadmaps from smaller, specialized segments of markets and stripping away traditional expensive advertising channels, minimum inventory buy-ins, and sales commitments often required from retailers.

Those brands that really, really understand their shoppers must begin to explore voice now.

By adopting voice now, you could own thousands of answers that will help educate and influence shoppers. Voice only has one answer, not pages and pages of answers.

---

[19] *Say OK Google - Talk to Discovered Book - Nike Direct Play*

There are **no participation ribbons** given with voice (on smart speakers).

There's no opportunity for your competitors to catch up and take that top spot from your brand. Since you can't advertise on voice yet, your answer can't be displaced by an ad.

If I had to predict what is going to happen, it is going to be exactly like it is now, the Retailers or eTailers are going to give the brand with the biggest bank preference and you better believe it will benefit them before it benefits your brand. In fact, Amazon is testing ads to voice skills in product searches and Google is testing ads on Google assistant results. Amazon is beginning to test the waters with mobile ads too, potentially posing a huge threat to Google and Facebook[20].

This is a chance for your brand to innovate. This is a chance for your brand to lead. This is a chance for your brand to dominate and shape the customer experience for your industry.

This book is going to challenge the way you think about search and discovery. It may even make you uncomfortable with doing things that are not typically "the norm" for your brand. **I want you to be comfortable with being uncomfortable.**

---

[20] *Say OK Google - Talk to Discovered Book - Amazon mobile ads*

If you do follow a strategy and you execute well, you could have a future-proof advantage. One that your competition can't even begin to comprehend or even know where to start to try and beat you.

As you continue this journey, you will understand the next big wave of innovation that's here could completely shift your business and help you earn a place in the hearts and minds of your shoppers in a very natural and engaging manner.

THE BUMPY ROAD OF ADAPTATION

My mom was not the typical suburban housewife. She was actually the furthest thing from it.

She was born in the 1930s and her mother died of tuberculosis when she was a baby, then her father remarried (to a woman who never wanted children) and he was killed in World War II. By the age of 5, she was forced to live with a stepmother and step-grandmother who wanted nothing to do with her. She grew up in a home with no love and often very cruel physical and mental abuse. She did what any smart 15-year-old girl did in the '40s. She dropped out of high school and married the cutest blonde hair blue eyed Italian boy she could find.

By the age of 20, my mom had three kids, no high school diploma, and a drunk and abusive husband. At that time in the United States, your husband was your legal guardian until you were 21 and most women wouldn't dare leave their husbands in the '50s anyway. But my mom was no ordinary woman, she studied to get her GED late at night, petitioned the court for a divorce, found a job as a secretary and left her husband with three kids in tow. She worked multiple jobs at a time to make enough money to feed her kids and did the best she could for a young mother. She kept interview records and performance reviews from her jobs back in the '50s and '60s and almost every job mentioned that she did not have a husband and tending to three kids could interfere with her ability to perform as well as her attendance.

My mom knew she made mistakes. Having children while we are still children cannot be an easy path to travel. I was actually the "do over" kid. I was adopted by my Mom when she was in her 40s. Her kids were grown and had their own families and lives. She had taken her savings, bought a house and was ready to love a child and give them a good life. That lucky little bundle of joy was me.

I was a child that was deemed "unadoptable" due to my unfortunate circumstances. Honestly, the word UNADOPTABLE was stamped on the outside of my manila file folder at the adoption agency. My birth mother's circumstances almost paralleled those of my adopted mother in that she too lived in a house with two people who chose not to love her. They didn't even notice her on most days, even to the point that she hid her pregnancy from her mother until she was almost nine months pregnant.

If we take our fate at face value, I should have remained unadoptable and grown up with the other 400,000 kids in the foster care system. The broken U.S. foster care system produces[21].

- Trauma so terrible that 25% of foster kids suffer from PTSD;
- 70% pregnancy rate in women under 21;
- 20% homelessness rate for kids that age out of the system at 18;
- Less than 3% ever get a college degree.

I could have been in a system which leads to terrible odds of abuse, addiction, crime, and much worse. With only a high school degree, I should have, by all accounts, been defeated. I should have just assumed the position that everyone else had in mind for me. But I didn't.

---

[21] Say *OK Google - Talk to Discovered Book - Foster kids need us*

You are faced with the same choice; do you stay where you are or do you:

- Begin to achieve better results?
- Begin to inspire and motivate your team with time to create, ideate, experiment, fail, and succeed?
- Accomplish the impossible?
- Engineer greatness?
- Love your career and reignite your passion for your work?
- Fulfill your desire to be transformative with your brand?

You have a choice. We can choose to stay complacent and accept things as they are or refuse to just exist.

Or we can create something legendary. Create experiences that transform our relationship with our shoppers.

INNOVATION AND TECHNOLOGY

When I started building websites two decades ago, the ugliest site in the world would get TONS of web traffic. And I am talking MySpace ugly. Busy backgrounds with so many colors it looked like a rainbow threw up. Bright yellow, highlighted sentences appeared too many times on the page, sometimes with bold red text. And don't forget the flashing banners. The ugliness could go on and on. You might as well whip out your stir-up pants, crushed velvet button-down shirt, and your Sony Walkman and come to the website disco par-tay!

Then, something strange happened: sales started to decline and the phones stopped ringing. Just having a website was not enough anymore. We had to evolve to stand out.

We learned to redesign websites so they wouldn't cause epileptic seizures and used these amazing new things called sliders. It was wonderful because now we could have more value propositions and different tag-lines that refresh every five seconds with a new image of the world's happiest people enjoying life (not necessarily at all related to what we sell). We could continue to give people so much more information. That's not confusing at all, right?

Enter the world of content. Content was the newest thing. Once we learned that "Content was king and consistency ruled the nation," we shifted gears once again. The beauty about content is it can be about ANYTHING. It can be about stubbing your toe when you got out of bed at 2 a.m. while having a ~~nightmare~~ dream about creating more content!

The content was supposed to keep visitors on websites longer, whether or not it was relevant, useful, and valuable. All we cared about was typing 250 words to publish that damn blog every Tuesday morning. Done and done!

That did the trick and luckily my phone started to ring again until... it didn't. Apparently, there are 3 million blog posts published a day, and I thought my blog is pretty awesome and way better than the other 2,999,999 websites publishing content, too. Again, not so much.

Perplexed and exhausted from making up crap every week to publish on my website, now something else has changed? Ugh. What the heck? I thought I nailed the magic formula with content and consistency.

I learned that content is still super important, but there is this thing called SEO (Search Engine Optimization), which helps people find my content when they are searching for an answer online.

I was intrigued until I read what felt like millions of blog posts with crappy advice, most of which I spent hours or days trying to find, that didn't work at all. I learned enough about SEO to know that I needed keyword-rich titles that someone was actually searching for as opposed to my killer blog title, "I think my dog ate a food bomb that exploded out of his @ss." What do you mean people aren't Googling that term and will immediately want to buy technology consulting from that amazingly descriptive, heartfelt, warm story about when my dog ate something that made his poop shoot out of his bottom like a rocket? Mind. Blown.

Then I had to master the complexity and many moving pieces of the SEO puzzle. It took years and years to understand it is much more than just a title or one keyword. It's a practice and methodology that needs to be followed and adapted as our human search behavior changes and consumer research, discovery, and buying journeys evolve.

In January 2018, it was estimated that there are over 1.69 billion websites[22]. Considering there are an estimated 3.8 billion people running 3.5 billion Google searches a day[23]. SEO is one of the most important factors in determining whether or not your website ever gets found at all.

I have traveled from the world of crappy websites to mobile-responsive, lightning-fast, retina-friendly websites. I have seen the lands of irrelevant 250-words blog posts to 2,000 words of insightful, time-saving, killer conversion copy-focused content. I have evolved from cute, witty, catchy but irrelevant titles to SEO-friendly, eyeball-worthy, and relevant titles. I have changed my mindset from getting 250 words to spit out on a screen to focusing on relevance as well as saving people time and money with valuable insight. And guess what? All of that still wasn't enough.

It took me a long time to realize my website wasn't supposed to be about me or my business, it was supposed to be about my prospect or my customer. *SAY WHAAAAAAAT*? For the last decade, it's always been about *me* and now we have to make it about *them*.

My website has to be about my customers, not me, but it has to be mobile-friendly and fast. The images have to be small and responsive. My sliders won't fit on a five-inch smartphone screen. Finally, the death of the sliders. Thank you, Google-verse!

Just as our lives and our businesses evolve, so does human behavior and technology. To think that what we were doing five years ago, no, six months ago, on our website is relevant and will result in sales today is like thinking you can watch a high-definition YouTube video on a neon purple Conair house phone with caller ID screen. It ain't gonna happen.

---

[22] *Say OK Google - Talk to Discovered Book - Number of websites*

[23] *Say OK Google - Talk to Discovered Book - Number of searches*

Chasing changing consumer behavior is like a moving target at a dog race. You will never win. So, how do you become the hunted and stop being the hunter? There are many opinions on techniques, methodologies, and proven practices. All of which I am sure work and move the needle slightly. But you are still the hunter with these.

The only way that I have consistently seen the roles reverse is by having an innovative culture that embraces emerging technology. Leveraging emerging technology can give you a leg up on your competition and leave everyone else scrambling trying to catch up. Innovation is not just a core value or something you "say" you do. It's the thread of the fabric of your mindset and your culture. It is an environment that fosters and supports creativity, ideation, and experimentation.

It's doing something that hasn't been done before: This means that there is no proven methodology, best practices, or historical data to support you because it really hasn't been done before.

Innovation can be some scary stuff, especially if you are risk-averse or your company culture avoids taking action based on risk or return. How do you know if your company supports innovation?

There are a couple of surefire signs that help us know whether or not your culture will support innovative thinking:

- Your company is open to validate assumptions.
- Your company prefers to make decisions based on data or facts, as opposed to past experience, gut, or bias.
- Your company encourages experimentation to test hypotheses or assumptions.
- Your company encourages creative or divergent thinking or out-of-the-box thinking.

- Your company tries new and different things, even without data, proof, certainty, or confidence that it will work.
- Your company is always curious.
- Your company is always learning.
- Your company accepts (not tolerates) failure.
- Your company runs tests or experiments and pivots quickly, meaning you aren't running the same test over and over, without changing anything, and expecting different results (again, the definition of insanity).
- Your team has the ability to pivot and respond quickly.
- Your company seeks out creative thinkers and recognizes when people aren't creative thinkers.
- Your leadership team is coachable, open to learning, and open to being wrong.

Whew! You may be looking at this list and realizing that your company may not have any of these traits. That's actually common and you're no exception. You don't have to possess every single trait on this list to be innovative but recognizing what could potentially cause you fail is a level of awareness that is necessary to play this game.

Innovation is a culture and mindset.

It is a philosophy that can be easily forgotten when you have a real job, with real pressures, and real metrics that real people are looking at your team to deliver. Innovation is something that can be frustrating, especially when you are trying new things – new things that took your team months to ideate, fine tune, and test, new things that could change the trajectory of your business forever.

Innovation is especially frustrating when it costs time or money, and doesn't yield immediate rewards and returns.

It is counter-intuitive to how most businesses have operated for decades.

Innovation can be hard to measure. Innovation can't be predicted with 100% certainty. It is often seen as risky. It is bold. And if it were easy, more people would be doing it.

Yes, it is challenging. But it can be so much fun to create something new, to shape an industry, to change the way people see, hear, engage, or interact with your brand. Innovation can bring smiles to the faces of little girls and boys, or grown-up girls and boys. You believe in your brand. You want to make the world a better place. If no one can find and experience your brand the moment they need you, how will you fully reach your brand's potential? But if you innovate well, the rewards could be priceless.

You may have a brand that was a leader, has lost market share to new emerging companies or technology, which has resulted in losing your mojo internally. Perhaps, you have only tried to do what you have always done, but better by iterating with incremental or no improvements. Innovation can be the one thing that brings your brand back to life, gives it relevance again, gets in front of the Millennials, Gen Zs, or any other target you're chasing.

Innovation can help you create an unbreakable bond with your customers, one that is so strong that shoppers become disciples for your brand advocating it to their friends and families until they purchase your products, too. Innovation can deepen the relationship between you and your customers by delivering a memorable, share-worthy experience that people can't stop talking about.

The second part of the equation is technology. I don't believe that technology and innovation are the same thing. Innovation is the invention of something new whereas technology is often the vehicle that enables innovation. They're like the Wonder Twins when they activate (aka fist bump).

Technology is a topic that could be its own series of encyclopedias. We didn't have time to look at encyclopedias when we were kids, so we certainly don't now. Technology has always been integrated into the waves of the future. And some of the technologies that we'll talk about in greater detail later may seem futuristic but they aren't at all. Every technology we discuss in this book is actively being developed, has already been developed, or is being used today.

People think that technology changes so fast, you just can't keep up with it. That is partly true. The pace in which we are creating things, from technology to product prototypes, has increased exponentially.

Other technologies can extend augmented reality and virtual reality to truly combine the digital and physical world of retail. In his book, "Reengineering Retail: The Future of Selling in a Post-Digital World," Doug Stephens talks about a new technology being built that will allow people to touch and feel a product before purchasing it[24]. Now, I am a total geek but that was something I'm still processing.

We need the basic technology that we use to run our lives but if you marry innovative thinking with emerging technologies, your brand can become an unstoppable force. You become the team, the coach, and the umpire. You make your own rules to the game and the stands have no more tickets for sale.

Just to be clear, the technology we will explore together is not the same software that everyone else is using, like Google Analytics or a Facebook Pixel. We are talking about the software many companies could be using but it isn't even on their radar because they may not know it exists. And if you are like the other 99.7% of brands that are still trying to be discovered on search, on social, or on

---

[24] Say *OK Google - Talk to Discovered Book – Reengineering Retail*

Amazon, then you're probably pretty consumed with everything that goes along with that stuff to even notice what we're going to talk about.

Technology is an investment but one that could reap rewards for many, many years, however, you might have to change the way you think about technology. Technology is the 8 speed (yes, gears go up to 8 now) in your Chevy ZR1, which is zero to 60 in 3.3 seconds car. If you don't know how to drive a manual transmission or a stick, you won't even pull out of the parking lot. You have access to performance race cars and no longer have to struggle to get out of first gear. It's time to go 0 to 60 in 3.3 seconds.

If your business is not embracing technology, especially when it comes to marketing online, you may not only miss the opportunity to grow your company, but also the opportunity to create memorable experiences, relationships, and customer loyalty that will be hard to displace.

Please make sure your seat belt is fastened and your tray tables and seat backs are in their upright and locked position because we are about to take off!

SECTION 1:
SEARCH

IMAGINE A WORLD

Imagine spending a nice relaxing weekend at home with the kids. You have told the kids that you are not spending any time doing work and they are not spending any time on anything with a screen. In my house, this is called "screen time." Screen time is anything with a screen and a power button. Screen time used to be a privilege, one that a child had to qualify for. That could mean they did something kind without being asked. They could finish their chores without being reminded 4,912 times. Perhaps they spent a lot of time on homework and I took pity on their soul. It ***used*** to be something that was a reward.

I started to notice that I was relying more and more on those evil screens, just so I could finish up a project or to take a late-night call with a client. It became *my crutch*, which turned into their addiction. I don't use the term addiction lightly. For any parent that has experienced the wave of video games like Minecraft, Roblox, and now Fortnite, it totally IS an addiction, one which I can't expect a kid to be able to control.

After the brutal reality that my reliance on technology as a babysitter is a very unhealthy one, we had to put limits on screen time again.

Back to your imaginary weekend filled with joy and bliss and scenes of happy togetherness. You spend what seems like five hours playing board games, Uno and Phase 10. You realize, OMG it has only been 26 minutes!

You decide to cook a meal as a family. Again, you have these grand visions of the kids loving this experience, which will be burned into their brains as The Best Weekend of my Childhood EVER!

You pick a meal that is not only healthy, but everyone can have a part in. You have cleaning duties for the little one. You have given the tween a knife with cutting duties. And you are on cooking duty.

After about three minutes and four seconds, the little one is out. He is over it and must retreat to sitting in his room staring at a blank TV screen because clearly, that is so much better than spending quality time with your family preparing a nutrient-rich meal. The tweenager is complaining about school, homework, and having a philosophical discussion with you about why Algebra has no real meaning in life and she doesn't understand why they have to learn certain things in school, anyway.

You aren't prepared for a philosophical conversation and you can't Google, "What does Algebra affect in our daily lives" because of your own stupid no screen time rule, so you try to "Uh huh" your way through as much as possible and continue to let her express her own opinions.

You have a meal with half-cleaned food, one half of a carrot since the onion is too much for delicate young girl eyeballs and nothing is ready to eat an hour later. At this point, everyone is frustrated and hangry, hungry + angry - thank you, Snickers.

You're beyond done. You just can't. You're not sure if this is what your kids are really like or are you being punked?

You whip open your laptop, only for the boy's sonic hearing owl ears who seemed to be instantly teleported into the kitchen to see if the no screen time rule is over. Your daughter is comparing you to the hypocrisy of the school system and teachers. This is why Calgon was created, for moments just like this one right now.

You Google search "Family Friendly events near me NOW."

The results that appear on the screen are colorful imagery and videos. You can see visual categories pictured at the top.

- Movies
- Parks
- Concerts
- Fairs
- Crafts

Being a busy working parent that you are, you have no idea what is in the movies but you do know there is most likely something in the theatres the kids want to see, so you click Movies.

This opens a new page of highly visual and engaging content. Along the top of the search page, you are given a visual display of the movies that are playing in theatre today.

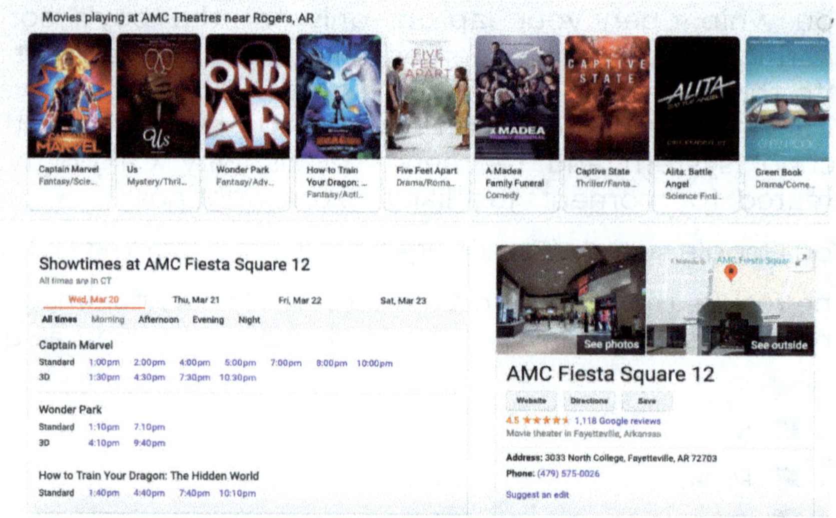

Source: My PC while in Bentonville, AR (Google knows everything...)[30]
Say OK Google - Talk to Discovered Book - Movies

In the middle of the page, showtimes, the nearest movie theatre, reviews, address, phone number, hours, and a map appear.

Within one simple search, out of sheer desperation to protect your sanity and the well-being of your children, you have found a way to help everyone survive the weekend.

What actually happened was you were able to get the answer to your question, very easily without clicking on five different websites. And just like that, you went from super annoying mom to best mom ever.

Thank you, Internet Gods.

What you may not have realized is all of that highly visual, rich, engaging content was provided by one brand: AMC wanted you to have all of the movie information you needed without ever having to click a single link.

Wait, what?! We want people to CLICK on our websites. Isn't that why the Internet was built in the first place?

This may seem like some futuristic search magic but it is actually what happens when brands optimize their experiences for questions and answers and intent using semantics. Semantics is a fancy way of saying meaning. By understanding the meaning of what people are searching for, you can fulfill their intent and give people an amazing brand experience starting with the search discovery process. This extends beyond online search into the voice search, voice assistants, and the smart speaker world

"People don't buy what you sell,
they buy how you sell it."

-Doug Stephens

THE EVOLUTION OF SEARCH

"You can't connect the dots looking forward; you can only connect them looking backwards."

– Steve Jobs

Before we can predict the future, we should try to learn from the past.

Anyone who remembers a day without Windows and a mouse recalls my roots in the 1980s. The good old days of great music, leg warmers, Aqua Net, 411 on hot pink Conair phones, floppy discs, dot matrix printers, and yes, even green screens.

Fast forward to the early 2000s and we have entered into the golden area of websites. There is a new company called Google that wants to put AOL and Ask Jeeves out of business. HA!

This new thing was introduced called an iPhone. It's supposed to be a "smartphone" (sarcastic air quotes), which ironically just made every slider in the world look like crap. Not so smart after all, eh?

Luckily, we won't be defeated with another disruptive change, so we entered the world of mobile responsiveness, which turns into a mobile-first design, which is now turning into voice-first design, which technically has nothing to do with my website, right? Wrong. It is the basis of everything on your website.

Mind. Blown. Again.

My entire career has been built upon knowing new technology before everyone else does. And translating those emerging technologies into value for our clients. Anticipating the next wave is tough work, but boy, is it fun!

Over the past couple of decades, we have experienced a few major waves of innovation:

- Windows
- Personal computing
- The internet
- Big data
- Smartphones

Every new wave of innovation presents us with both new challenges and new opportunities.

Opportunities to:

- Validate our riskiest assumptions
- Improve customer buying journeys
- Offer more personalized experiences
- Provide easier ways to find and buy our products
- Develop ways to create relationships with our customers

Now, it's not all rainbows and unicorns. We now live in a world of "Too."

Too much data

First, we didn't have any data, then we had big data, now we have too much data yet we don't feel like we have enough insight from all of this data to actually take action and do anything with it.

Too many software providers

There are more than 7,000 technologies focused on JUST MARKETING! In. Sane.

Too many options

Pick any one Too's: Ads, social channels, influencers, media outlets, agencies, and thousands of other options. None of us have time or money to waste on things that won't move the needle. That's where innovation and emerging technologies can help us stand out in the online world of discovery and search.

Too much information

As the internet explodes into gazillions of websites, search engines are faced with the challenge of too much information. Some information is relevant and useful and some is meaningless.

Just as we have too many options in business with software and data, search engines also have too many options with answers to search questions.

Just as we evolved, so do the search engines. We often lose site of the challenge that comes with managing data and delivering a great experience. It's not easy.

From this point on, I challenge you to think of search engines as *discovery engines*. The job of discovery engines has become one of responding to questions to help people discover the right answer. People are also starting to call search engines *answer engines*. We are busy people with no time or patience to field through pages of links. We want the right answer now and we expect it to be delivered at the top of page 1!

"The core of what Google is about is bringing information to people."

– Sundar Pichai

You will hear me reference Google often because Google is focused on delivering the ultimate customer experience. We will focus on what to optimize to improve search. When they update their algorithm, it is for the sole purpose to improve the customer's experience. Although it can be frustrating it is important for the good of humanity, search humanity that is.

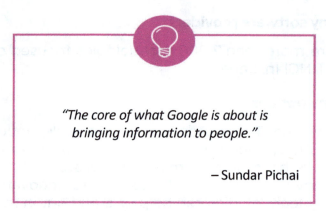

Our intent may be the same, to eat dinner. But I know my kids like the most expensive thing on the menu and I want to find a restaurant that has happy hour food specials. Meanwhile, your intent might be to find a restaurant that doesn't have a happy hour so you can enjoy a peaceful dinner (without screaming kids). I get it. I was that person too.

Bottom line is we may both search. We may both have the intent to find a restaurant. Our preferences are totally different. Brands that take the time to really understand the intent their people have will win more hearts, minds, and dollars.

"Intent" is a common buzzword, but that doesn't mean people know what to do about it, or even where to start. And it's actually not that hard at all. A good place to start is by validating intent with real people, the right real people.

The Buying Power of Women

I'm not sure whether or not your brand sells to men or women. The buying power of women is incredible. Most consumer brands sell to women. The way that women buy is *totally* different than the way that men buy. Unintentionally, I spent the last 10 years working with consumer brands that sell to women, which is ironic because I hate shopping. But now I understand the psychology of what influences the decision-making process and points of friction during the buying journey.

Many of us don't recognize how much psychology is involved in purchase decisions.

Regardless of what you sell, there is always an emotional aspect to everything! Even if you have the cold, hard facts about why someone should buy your product, a majority of the time the decision is 90% emotional and 10% logical. Another dynamic that you have to understand is when you sell to women, sometimes you have to overcome subconscious objections. A perfect example of this is feeding our kids.

Whether you manage your household, a career, an organization, or your life, you are probably pretty busy. Imagine you are a working parent and for whatever reason, you are overscheduled again today. You have to get one kid from soccer and another kid to Jiu Jitsu -- another 7 a.m. to 9 p.m. day. Woohoo. At some point between school and bedtime, you have to feed your kids dinner.

Back in the day you might pull up to a drive-thru and pick up happy meals. At some point, we became more self-conscious and health-conscious of the food that we feed our children and too many nights of McDonald's drive-thru dinners made us feel like bad parents. We're all familiar with the feeling of "Mommy Shame" or "Daddy Guilt." After we feed unhealthy meals to our kids, we feel bad. Consciously, you might not realize what makes you feel the way but you are just in a crappy mood now. You feel like you're not providing for your kids. You aren't being a good caregiver. You're aren't teaching your kids healthy habits. No one said this to you, you just feel it in your soul.

We want to cook healthy yummy nutritious meals that your family enjoys but the time and effort to plan the meal is more than we make the time for.

This is how it normally works:

- Decide what you are going to cook
- Find "quick recipes for healthy dinners for 4"
- Print the recipes
- Study the list of ingredients
- See what you have in the pantry that is on the ingredients of the multiple recipes
- FINALLY, make a grocery list
- Go to the grocery store
- Buy all the stuff you need
- Meal prep (look up #mealprep on Instagram)
- When the time comes, prepare your glorious meal.
- Your family feels loved, provided for, and grows up to be healthy functioning adults.

Who has time for that? Not busy parents. So, what do we do instead?

- Feed our kids mac and cheese and chicken fingers (way too often)
- Let them eat snacks or cereal for breakfast (way too many nights a week)
- Eat out or order food delivery (way too expensive)
- Sign up for a meal box subscription

For many of us this is a huge emotional trigger and challenge in our lives but what a freaking opportunity for meal prep delivery companies, right?

Black Buying Power

It is often easy to focus on demographics and ignore some of the more obvious traits, like race. But I am going to keep it real for everyone else's sake. Black buying power is real and it is major. Black culture influences culture around the world, whether you haven't noticed or you choose to believe it or not. It dates back before our time to music, when black music, even when not allowed was enjoyed by all colors, shapes, sizes, and backgrounds. Black culture continues to influence young women, kids, and major networks. Fox has a category called "Urbantainment" which includes shows like "Empire" and "Star." I was surprised to find out that the most watched reality show on television was "Love & Hip Hop Atlanta," series on VH1 not "The Real Housewives" series on Bravo TV. From music to slang, to fashion, to sports, and more there is an undeniable connection to our world and black influence.

What does that mean for your brand? If your brand markets to women, then can't avoid, ignore, or exclude the black market. It is different. We have a different level of loyalty and brand affinity. Here are some data points from Nielsen's Report: "Black Girl Magic" and Brand Loyalty Is Propelling Total Black Buying Power Toward $1.5 Trillion by 2021[31].

- Black spending power is estimated to reach $1.5 trillion by 2021;
- Black women-owned businesses have grown by 67%, with more than 1.5 million businesses worth $42 billion in sales;
- Black women are trendsetters for consumerism and consumption;
- They seek to project a positive self-image and appreciate brands that do the same;
- They are brand LOYAL. And will slay your brand if they feel betrayed.

---

[31] Say *OK Google - Talk to Discovered Book – Black Buying Power*

> *"Black women have strong life-affirming values that spill over into everything they do. The celebration of their power and beauty is reflected in what they buy, watch and listen to, and people outside their communities find it inspiring."*
>
> -Cheryl Grace,
> Senior Vice President of U.S. Strategic Community Alliances and Consumer Engagement, Nielsen

Every brand should take the time to understand this demographic and read the report. There is a more comprehensive, science-based report about the psychology and behaviors of black women in Nielsen's African American Women: Our Science, Her Magic[32].

In fact, a dear friend of mine, Kalyn Johnson Chandler starting selling Black Girl Magic swag before black women were considered a desired and affluent target market for brands. She created what has now become an iconic logo; it's ethereal ... just like we are – beautiful, powerful and resilient. Women are drawn to her Black Girl Magic logo because it hits the mark. It gives black women permission to stop hiding their magic and display it proudly. While well known for her Black Girl Magic products, her brand is inclusive and focuses on female empowerment, she's got a great tag line: "We believe the future is female and is being fueled by Black Girl Magic!" To check out her products (in my opinion, she's got some of the best Black Girl Magic swag out there) visit her online store at www.EffiesPaper.com and social feeds at @effiespaper.[33]

Don't target this market if you do not have an authentic brand voice. Don't hire someone to do an "ethnic

---

[32] Say *OK Google - Talk to Discovered Book – Black Girl Magic*

[33] Say *OK Google - Talk to Discovered Book – Effie's Paper*

campaign" and check it off your list. Either authentically play and participate or don't. Black women are **vocal** with likes and more so with dislikes. When black owned brand Shea Moisture was acquired by Dove, they launched a campaign #AllHairMatters. Dove was eager to increase other ethnicities, besides black, which had been the primary demographic. Dove may not have realized how touchy the BlackLivesMatter issue was to Black people. Nor could they anticipate the upset a picture of White women in an authentic Black brand would cause. The backlash was real...real ugly[34]. It took months to try to repair the damage from one poorly messaged campaign. You don't have to go in All Black or Not Black but you need to understand the culture, the values, and expectation from us before you release a premature initiative.

Affluent and Underserved

The last demographic I want to highlight is often underserved but affluent is the Baby Boomers. They are the ones who created the Advertising Age, yet so many brands are worried about them "aging out" and have completely shifted away from marketing to them at all beyond 55. This could be a misstep for some brands where Boomers are still a clear fit and have the problems, will pay to solve them, and have the discretionary income to do so.

Here are some interesting stats about Boomers[35]

- There are 74.9 million Baby Boomers in the US alone spend $3.12 trillion per year, which is greater than the GDP the UK, Italy, Russia, Brazil and France!
- Baby Boomers control the most net worth (39%) and

[34] Say *OK Google - Talk to Discovered Book – All Hair Matters*

[35] Say *OK Google - Talk to Discovered Book – Selling to Baby Boomers*

the most total income (34%);

- Baby Boomers account for 50% of all consumer expenditures;
- Less than 10% of marketing spend targets people over the age of 50;
- 77 million Baby Boomers are on social media;
- They read! Email (Average open rate - 90%);
- They click! Promotions, email offers, online (Average rate again - 90%+);
- They love mail. Yes, snail mail (direct mail);
- They want information, engagement, and value from their brands;
- They love to spend money on other people;
- They are active online shoppers who are becoming more and more tech savvy, especially on voice.

Underestimating Emotion

If you've ever seen leadership expert Simon Sinek's TED Talk "Start with Why," then you may understand how important this is.

To be quite frank, there probably isn't much difference between the product that you offer and the product your competitors are selling. Maybe there's a couple tiny things that you do better but all and all, if someone's trying to solve the problem, it can probably be done by your brand or your competitions.

This is where emotion matters the most. As consumers create these personal, intimate relationships with brands, emotions will be a factor. It's hard enough to sell, now we have to understand how the subconscious affects purchasing behavior...great!

According to Harvard Business School professor Gerald Zaltman says that 95% of purchasing decisions happen with the subconscious mind[36].

> *"When marketing a product to a consumer, it's most effective to target the subconscious mind."*
>
> – Gerald Zaltman

In Zaltman's latest book, "How Customers Think: Essential Insights into the Mind of the Market," he delves into the subconscious mind of the consumer—the place where most purchasing decisions are made[37]. He states there are a couple of things marketers may consider when learning about how this affects the purchasing behavior of shoppers:

- Verify what people state are beliefs with their actual behavior.
- Understand what shoppers say when asked directly versus how they behave when they actually are purchasing may be different.
- Study metaphors they express through thoughts and feelings through probing deeper in one-on-one interviews for hidden meanings. Something we often look for in tonality, sentiment, and body language when we perform Voice of Customer interviews.

Don't discount conscious and subconscious triggers, objections, and friction points during the journey. And if possible, validate what people say versus what they actually do.

---

[36] Say *OK Google - Talk to Discovered Book – Emotional Selling*

[37] Say *OK Google - Talk to Discovered Book – How Customers Think*

Millennial Behavior Changes the Game

Many brands are scrambling trying to understand how to shift from older demographics to younger ones (i.e., Baby Boomer to Millennials). Let's examine a brand with a demographic that may be "aging out." A perfect example is in the marine or recreational watercraft (aka boats) industry. Their primary demographic was typically an older 40s, going into the later stages of life, not necessarily baby boomer age but right before retirement age. Their behavior is changing as that demographic isn't spending the same money on boats. They have to pay fees to store a boat, clean the boat, maintain the boat, and dock the boat. If this is your primary demographic and your main source of revenue, that is a huge risk, since your entire industry is built upon one demographic that isn't necessarily interested in the same products they were 10-15 years ago.

If your brand decides to shift from an older demographic to a younger demographic, like Millennials, then you must begin to understand how EQ, emotion, and psychology affects your connection with Millennials and future generations.

In the Adobe/ Invoca Report, Emotions Win: What Customers Expect in the Age of AI, there's a ton of great info about how Millennials vs Baby Boomers, Men vs Women, Gen X vs Gen Y want and expect to interact and engage with brands[38]. Millennials would prefer to interact with brands that have a certain level of emotional quotient. Emotional Quotient is defined as the ability to recognize and respond to their emotional state. When asked about what is most important characteristics of interacting with a brand, they replied:

---

[38] Say *OK Google - Talk to Discovered Book – Millennials and Brands*

- 90% want problem-solving
- 89% want to support
- 84% want an even temper
- 75% expect personalization

Customer Experience Wins

It's time to shift from less omnichannel and more omnipresent to help with discovery across hundreds of customer experience moments and touchpoints.

The customer experience is filled with so many different moments from discovery to decision of whether or not to trust and choose your brand.

These moments matter! You should truly try to understand what these moments are and what the consumer needs to hear, see, or feel, at that moment. Every one of these moments is an opportunity for your brand to shine in the eyes of the shopper. If you deliver the right information in the right way to help move them further along the journey in a valuable and meaningful way, then you are on the right track. Your job to fulfill the consumer's intent at that moment, to give the customer the insight and confidence that your brand is the right product to choose. They hear why. They see why. And most importantly, they feel why your brand is the brand that can solve their problems better than any other brand on the market.

At REI, the outdoor recreational equipment retailer, every decision, including which products to sell, are based on the customer buying journey[39]. And that journey is filled with moments of pain points and opportunities. Everything focuses on the moment to moment journey with their brand and the specific needs to be met in that

---

39 Say *OK Google - Talk to Discovered Book –REI*

moment. It's an opportunity to bring their customers to a specific place, online and offline, that delivers information each person needs to move further.

Brief encounters like searching for a store address to looking for a specific headlamp that is designed for temperatures below -20 degrees AND is waterproof are important to REI customers.

Think of people like a puzzle with many varied pieces, colors, sizes, and shapes, all of which have to fit together. Here are a few of the pieces of the puzzle:

- Behavior
- Intent
- Preferences
- Emotions
- Psychological triggers
- Values, passion, purpose

Understanding these characteristics together will help deepen your connection with your consumers when they are researching and discovering in search.

Use Case Example

Meet Morgan, a 40-year-old woman who has been struggling with fatigue and sleeplessness. She has searched for everything. She's tried countless sleep tricks, caffeine at different times of the day, and visits to her doctors.

After batteries of tests, she learns that as she aged, she has developed food sensitivities to many foods she used to love and now needs to learn to live without.

This opens up a new world of research and discovery. In her search of food sensitivities, she uncovers other terrifying facts that lead her to believe that she may have a predisposition for diabetes since she comes from a family of people plagued with diabetes and poor health.

She makes the decision that, starting today, she is going to eat healthy meals at home opposed to eating out so frequently.

Over the next several weeks, Morgan goes on a quest to learn and discover how to live her new life. Here are some of the ways she begins to search and discover:

- At work, she is hungry and resists the urge to hit the vending machine and buy her favorite trail mix with M&Ms snack. To keep her mind off the M&Ms, she searches for "How can I get rid of food cravings?"
- Morgan is sitting in the carpool line and she would normally be sipping her daily flat latte with one pump of caramel but since she is trying to cut back on coffee, she searches for "What can I drink that has less caffeine than coffee but still tastes like dessert?"
- While partly paying attention to the longest baseball practice ever, Morgan searches for, "Quick healthy low-carb dinners without gluten."
- Morgan often wakes up in the middle of the night and tries to fall back asleep but when she finds herself wide awake at 2 a.m., she searches for "What foods affect insomnia or cause fatigue?"

If you are a healthy food brand, your mission may be to help people live without processed, byproducts, and artificial ingredients. You feel like it is your job and responsibility to reach as many people as possible like Morgan, who is just starting to learn about healthier alternatives and the millions that aren't even aware that they should be living a healthier lifestyle.

- Could your brand answer these questions?
- Do you know the science of how food affects sleep?

- Would it be of value to educate and inform Morgan even if she doesn't buy your meals right away?
- Could you use search or voice to nurture her through her journey of research and discovery?

Absolutely! This would build reciprocity, trust, authority, credibility, and affinity. This information could provide Morgan peace of mind and could begin a meaningful relationship with your potential shopper.

This is one example of the utility of search and discovery and there are thousands of other use cases beyond this one.

IMPROVING DISCOVERY WITH SEARCH

"I call her Google because she's got everything I have been searching for."

— Genereux Philip

How It All Started

Back in 2011, the major search engines and information providers like Google, Yahoo, Yandex, and Microsoft came together and agreed that the internet and their search consumers needed a better way to search. It was like Jekyll Island in 1931 but for the Internet. If you haven't heard about what happened in Jekyll Island, and you like reading really big books, you should check out the book by G. Edward Griffin, "The Creature from Jekyll Island: A Second Look at the Federal Reserve," which talks about how the largest privately held banks and richest families from around the world (i.e., the Rockefellers, Rothchilds, etc.) formed the Federal Reserve in the United States[45]. It is some craziness.

Back to 2011. From those meetings with the leaders of information, Schema Markup was created and Schema.org was born. Schema.org is a third party, not owned or influenced by any specific search provider. The entire purpose of Schema is to provide a unified answer.

[45] Say *OK Google - Talk to Discovered Book – Jekyll Island Craziness*

Schema.org is the global vocabulary of information, which is often used as the source for many search and discovery engines. Schema.org helps tell the internet what your brand's website means, not just what your web pages say. And there is a very distinct difference.

Schema.org gives more structure to information on the internet. This is called Structured Data, also sometimes referred to as Rich Snippets. By giving the data on the internet more structure, the discovery engines (or answer engines) understand the context behind the content. Context helps the discovery engines understand the meaning of your content or your brand.

Here are a couple of examples of before and after Schema

Web Page	Before Schema What it says?	After Schema What it means?
Home Page	Best ice cream	Our ice cream is a non-GMO, organic, sustainable ice cream that has been awarded the best ice cream since 2016. We are available now in 27 locations in the Atlanta area
Product Page	43" TV	43" TV - Latest plasma TV Awarded Best of 2019. Sold in Walmart, Best Buy, and Sam's Club. 4.8 stars, 1,879 Reviews, Specs, SKU, Dimensions, Inventory, Pick up now.
Recipes	BBQ Chicken Recipe	10 Minute BBQ Chicken Recipe - 4.9 stars - 551 reviews - 15 minutes - 220 calories
Reviews	Our customers love us! Check out our reviews.	Aggregate reviews, 4.75 stars, 5,397 reviews, customer service reviews, product reviews
Contact	Contact Us	We offer 24/7 Customer Service online chat. Service 888-555-2222, Sales 800-555-1111. Rated #1 for customer service for 4 years in a row by Conde Nast.

These are just a few of 830+ types of Schema Markup that can be applied to your brand's web pages. No matter what you sell, and to whom, there are techniques to leverage Schema for your brand that will set it apart from the rest.

To effectively win with online search today, we have to deliver rich, relevant data directly within search results. Using structured data, through Schema, you can organically dominate search results, giving you the prime Google Page One real estate above the fold.

SEO is still vitally important. Structured data does not replace SEO. The stronger your SEO game is, the better your chances are to make an incredible impact on your organic online presence with Schema. Schema can complement and supercharge your SEO efforts. Google is thirsty for more structured data content. We are seeing the speed of results appearing much faster in recent months as Google continues to identify and reward brands that are implementing structured data correctly.

According to a SearchMetrics study done for Google that analyzed more than 500 million websites, almost 30% of the websites had some form of rich snippets (or content), but less than .3% were actually doing Schema right.

Less than a ⅓ of 1%, not 3%. Of 500 million websites, less than 1.5 million sites were using Schema software properly[46].

---

[46] Say *OK Google - Talk to Discovered Book – Schema Research*

"We started building lots of new features that rely on structured data, kind of like we started caring more and more about structured data. That is an important hint for you if you want your sites to appear in search features Implement Structured Data."

Gary Illyes
Google Webmaster Trends Analyst
Pubcon, 2017

Navigating Search

Online search is tricky because it constantly changes. However, that's where it all begins with consumers: 84% of consumers start with search as the first step in research and discovery[3], and 90% of consumers said they use search at every stage of their customer buying journey[4].

When I talk about search, I often frame it around Google because if you optimize your site for Google, you will see rewards on the other search and answer engines, too. Google has made it very clear that they have very specific guidelines that they want brands and businesses to follow.

It's funny because Google will tell you exactly what they want you to do in order for them to view your site as trustworthy and credible. This is known in the industry as your EAT Rating; Expertise, Authority, and Trust.

Expertise | Authority | Trust

By understanding the factors to increase your EAT Rating, you can be ahead of 90% of your market.

Google's Guidelines are in plain sight and easily accessible[47]. These guidelines are updated as of May 16, 2019, and you can visit my website at Discovedbook.com/ Book for the link to the latest guidelines. The guidelines give you great detail about what you need to do to rank as an authoritative source in their search results. How Google ranks is not the mystery everyone claims it is.

It's way too long to read (166 pages) but if you want to learn more about it, Google explains it more simply on their site[48].

We're not going to dive into the hundreds of techniques that everyone else is doing based on Google's guidelines, rather, we are going to focus on one thing. It's one thing that 70% of brands haven't ever heard of, while the rest are crushing the Schema game. Ironically, in that 30% less than 0.3% are actually using Schema software properly[46].

Just to put the search opportunity into perspective, here are the numbers around the volume of search queries in general.

---

[47] Say *OK Google - Talk to Discovered Book – EAT*

[48] Say *OK Google - Talk to Discovered Book – Google Algorithms*

On just Google, there are more than:

- 40,000 searches per second
- 3.5 billion searches per day
- 1.2 trillion searches per year

I can't even process those numbers in my head rationally. Certain single search terms, like "best baby food" return more than 4 million search results[19]. Every result is competition for your brand. All of those sites are also attempting to be found online as the top answer on Google. Highly competitive terms result in more than 1 billion search results or other websites with similar keywords. If there are trillions of searches, the number of search results has to be a number I don't know how to pronounce.

If you want to see what Google searches look like, visit http://www.internetlivestats.com and click on the Google searches today ticker.

Nerdy facts moment:

- In 1999, it took Google one month to crawl and build an index of about 50 million pages. In 2012, the same task was accomplished in less than one minute.
- Up to 20% of queries that get asked every day have never been asked before.
- Every query has to travel, on average, 1,500 miles to a data center and back to return the answer to the user.
- A single Google query uses 1,000 computers in 0.2 seconds to retrieve an answer.

Crazy, right?

Benefits of Schema

Every single brand can benefit from Schema Markup. I don't care what you sell or who you sell to.

> Your business can **absolutely benefit** from implementing Schema properly.

Many of us struggle with continuing to pay more and more for ad spend only to get diminishing dismal results. Why would we continue to pay more money on ads to reach less people? Can you reduce those costs on your own right now? Absolutely!

Here are a couple of changes to make today:

- Tweak the copy.
- Change the creative.
- Change the button's color or placement.
- Change the call to action.
- Change the path to purchase or journey.

Most of these changes won't make enough difference to see a return on the time and money spent.

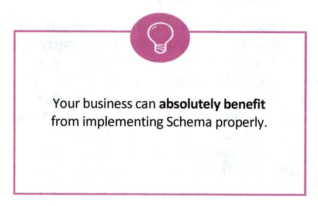

Why Schema?

Forty percent of consumers have an ad blocker on their desktop and 15% have them on mobile[49]. This number doubled in 2018. It has also been rumored that cell phone providers may start providing ad blocking capabilities built into the mobile devices core operating systems. This would give consumers more control over what they see and hide.

Ironically, consumers don't mind ads if the ad is relevant and they see the ad at the right time and in the right place. For instance, if the ad answers their question, they would be willing to watch the video or click the link or see your ad.

Unfortunately, many of us are still making assumptions about what the right ad is. If we make the wrong assumption, then people are just going to ignore our ads, which is a colossal waste of time and money.

Ads are not a long-term, sustainable strategy and for new brands, ads can give you a false sense of growth and traction, which is super risky early on. If we can grow organically and get that right, then that growth IS sustainable. Schema can help your brand create a sustainable path to growth.

When the Schema is done properly, you'll see more:

- Organic traffic
- Engagement with your site
- Engagement with your content
- Time spent on page
- Click-through rates

[49] Say *OK Google - Talk to Discovered Book – Ad Blockers*

- Clicks to pages
- Visits to pages

When more of the right people see your site, ultimately you will enjoy more transactions and sales.

Schema helps search engines, answer engines, and voice engines understand:

- The meaning of your brand
- The purpose of your brand
- The voice of your brand
- The identity of your brand
- The points of differentiation of your brand
- The associations, distribution channels, and connections to your brand
- The utility of your brand
- The value behind your product
- Why people should buy your products

Google and others do the best they can to really understand your brand and the context of what your brand really means. They are piecing together this massive web of keywords, content, touchpoints, connections, channels, and interactions. When we research a brand, we find Google partially understands the brand but often there is not enough semantic meaning for Google to paint the complete picture for our shoppers.

Nothing is more frustrating than spending precious resources creating amazing digital and web experiences, only to never be found by the people you are in business to serve in the first place.

With Schema, you are increasing your organic traffic and you are following the clues from Google. Your content is seen as more relevant, trusted, and credible in her eyes. And she will reward you handsomely. Yes, Google is a she. No, I don't have proof. I just know things.

If you're a brand or retailer and you want to stand out, you should start focusing on Schema Markup, which provides a semantic layer to the website. Search engines are trying to understand how pages, brands, companies, and people are all connected.

When you do that well, you're making the jobs of little Google robots easier. The little Google robots will love you for it and reward your brand!

You understand better than anyone else:

- The connection between your brands and your channels
- The transformation of your customer's life before and after they use your products
- The core values of your organization that may align with the values of your customers
- The authenticity and voice of your brand
- The sustainability in your production process
- Your causes and contributions to the world

Simply stated, all you have to do is explain that or other relevant information to Schema and you get organic search brownie points. How amazing is that?

What is Schema Exactly?

I want you to imagine for a moment a wagon, like an old Western style wagon. Imagine you're traveling across the frontier with some screaming kids and two horses in an old-fashioned wagon. Think about the wheels on the wagon. They're these huge wooden wheels with spokes.

Assume that the center of the wheel, which is called the hub, is the brain.

The center of our wheel is our brain hub. The hub of the wheel holds everything together. Without the hub, we couldn't hold the spokes. Without the spokes, we couldn't connect to the outer rim of this wheel. Without the outer rim, our wheel couldn't roll. Without the wheel, the wagon couldn't move.

Just like the brain helps our bodies work better together, the brain hub of that wheel is where the wheel starts. The brain hub for the wheel is Schema.

Example of how Schema gives your web pages meaning[50]

Say OK Google - Talk to Discovered Book – Schema

Schema is the encyclopedia, the dictionary, the map, and the GPS. It's the navigator of everything. Each spoke is a page, an image, a video, a channel, a recipe, a review, platform, or an influencer. Each spoke is primed to be discovered for the question or the intent your shopper is trying to fulfill.

Schema allows you to help discovery engines to **understand your brand better so you get discovered by more of the right people**.

Schema is the connector between your brand and the millions of people searching for the solution that your brand solves better than any other company in the world.

Brands' Schema Examples

There are so many possibilities when it comes to Schema. If you are a brand that provides food, then a very common Schema type is recipes. Recipes appear as a visual preview of what the food looks like, the number of stars or rating, the number of people who have actually reviewed or rated the recipe, the minutes to prepare, and even the calories for the meal.

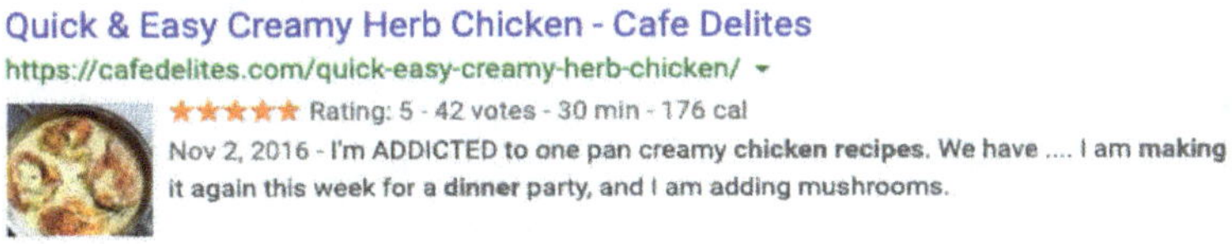

Quick & Easy Creamy Herb Chicken - Cafe Delites
https://cafedelites.com/quick-easy-creamy-herb-chicken/
★★★★★ Rating: 5 - 42 votes - 30 min - 176 cal
Nov 2, 2016 - I'm ADDICTED to one pan creamy chicken recipes. We have .... I am making it again this week for a dinner party, and I am adding mushrooms.

Source: Google Search Results Page[51]

Say OK Google - Talk to Discovered Book – Easy Creamy Herb Chicken

Visit Google's Developer site to see several examples of the various ways Schema appears in search results[52].

You have totally seen Schema before, you probably just never realized it had a name. Don't worry, you're not alone. If everyone knew about Schema, it wouldn't be your unfair advantage.

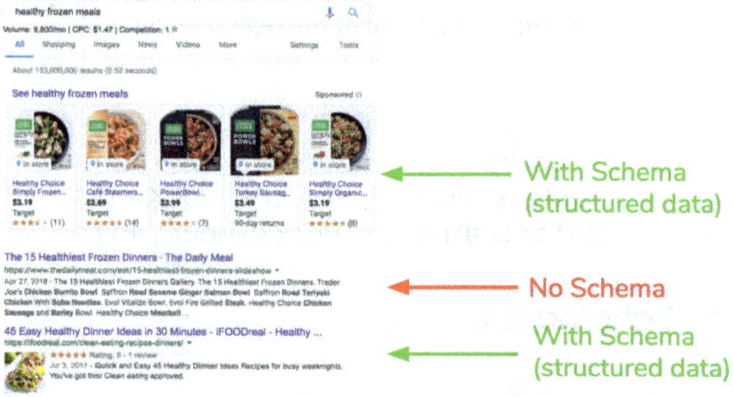

Common Types of Schema[53]

Say OK Google - Talk to Discovered Book – Schema Types

Since 2011, Schema.org has released 830+ different classes. Think of the class as a classification or type (of content or page). There are different types of pages and content such as:

- Articles
- Books
- Corporate Contacts
- Courses
- Jobs & Employee Reviews
- Events
- Fact Checking

---

[52] *Say OK Google - Talk to Discovered Book – Schema Results*

- Local Businesses
- Products
- Recipes
- Reviews
- Videos
- Q&A
- How To's

Schema about Your Business

Source: Google, Local Business[54]

Say OK Google - Talk to Discovered Book - Local Business

Schema about Your Products

A very common use of Schema is when you have multiple products and categories; then you can display your product features, specifications, pricing, availability, and reviews right there within the search results

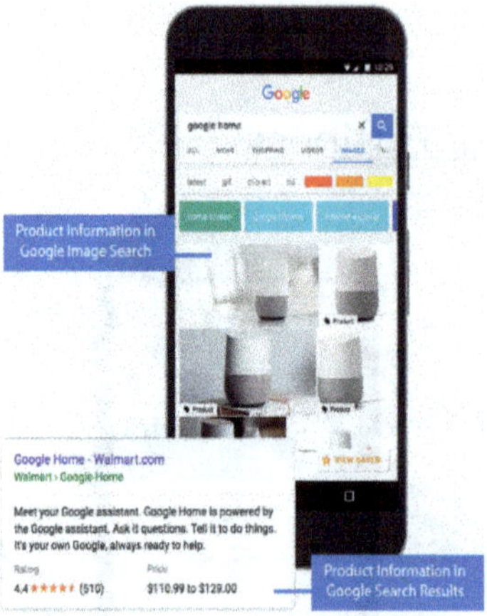

Source: Google, Products Images Search[55]

Say OK Google - Talk to Discovered Book – Product Images

Schema about Reviews and Ratings

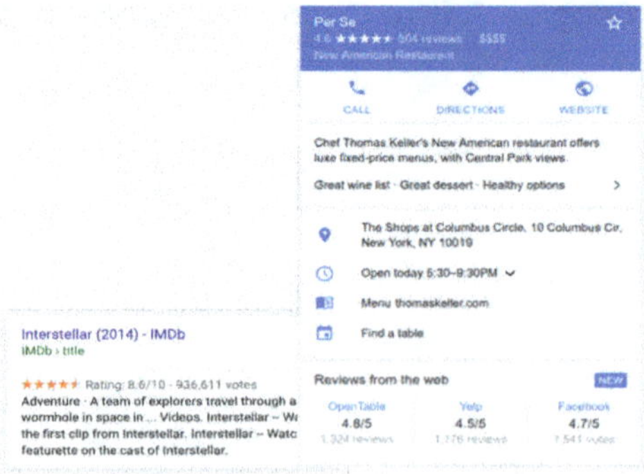

Source: Google, Reviews and Ratings[56]

Say OK Google - Talk to Discovered Book - Reviews

Schema about Your Events

If you are marketing events, traveling pop-up shows, in-store campaigns, or retail activations, then you may want to check out the event Schema. This example shows a concert tour with the concert cities, times, and even seat availability.

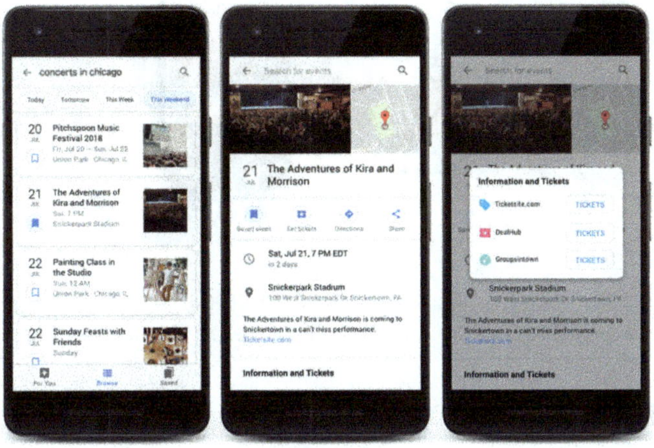

Source: Google, Events[57]

Say OK Google - Talk to Discovered Book - Events

Schema about Food and Recipes

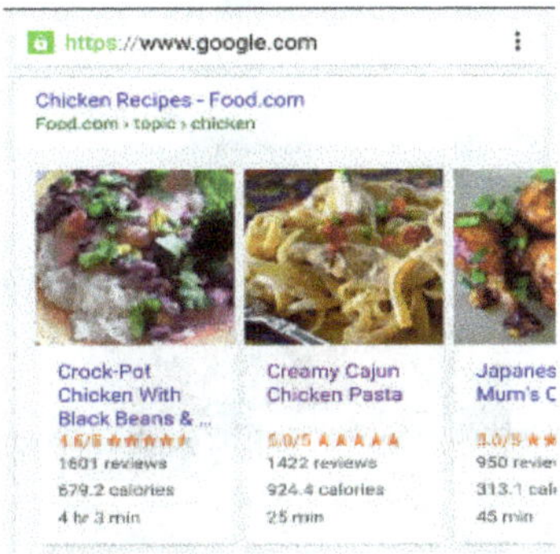

Source: Google, Carousel[58]

Say OK Google - Talk to Discovered Book - Carousel

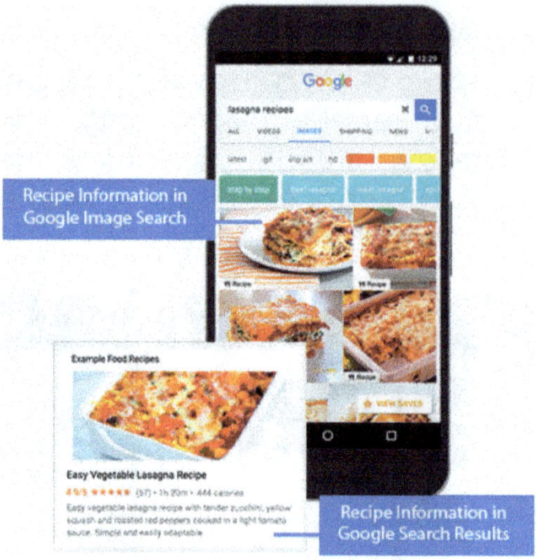

Source: Google, Recipes[59]

Say OK Google - Talk to Discovered Book - Recipes

Schema about Top Places List

Top places is in beta but shows up when someone search for "Top 10 Chinese restaurants in NYC."

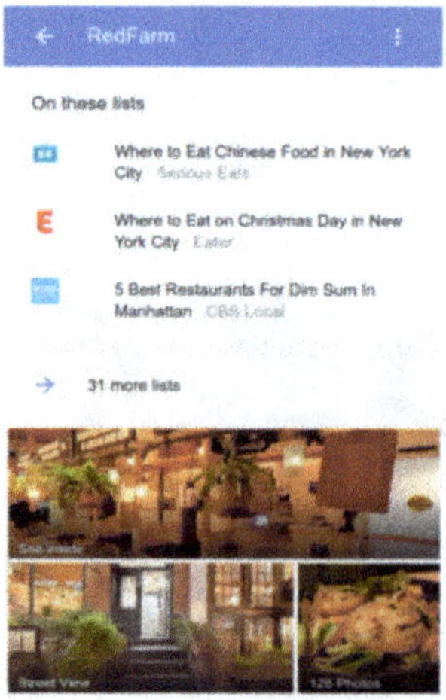

Source: Google Top Places List Example[60]

Say OK Google - Talk to Discovered Book – Top Places

Schema about Videos

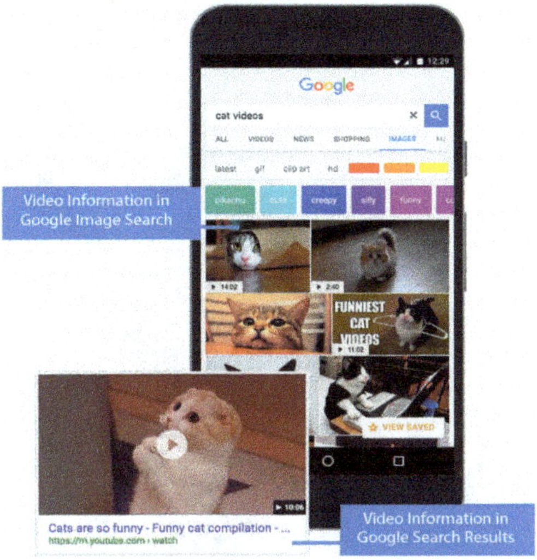

Source: Google, Videos[61]

Say OK Google - Talk to Discovered Book - Videos

Schema to answer Information, FAQ, and How To questions and searches

FAQs on Online Search

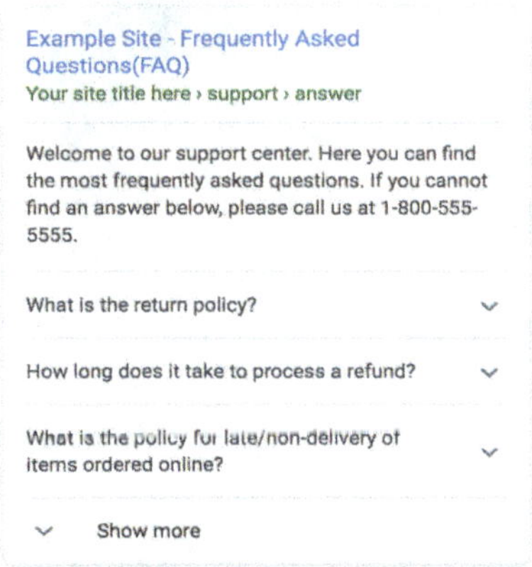

Source: Google, Online Search, FAQ Example[62]

Say OK Google - Talk to Discovered Book – FAQ Online Search

FAQs on Voice Assistant Search

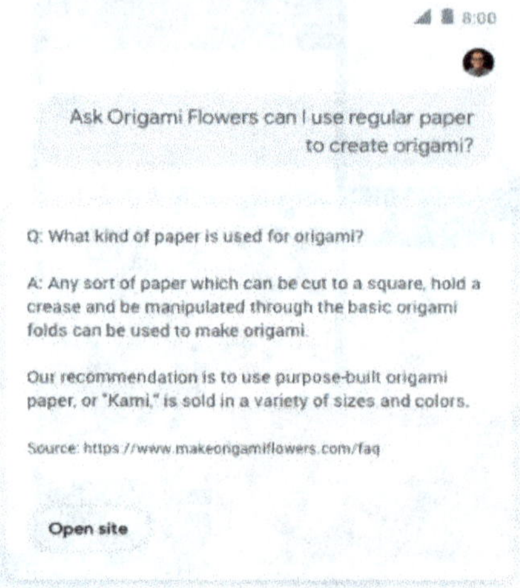

Source: Google, Voice Assistant Search, FAQ Voice Example[63]
Say OK Google - Talk to Discovered Book – FAQ Voice Search

How To's on Voice Assistant Search

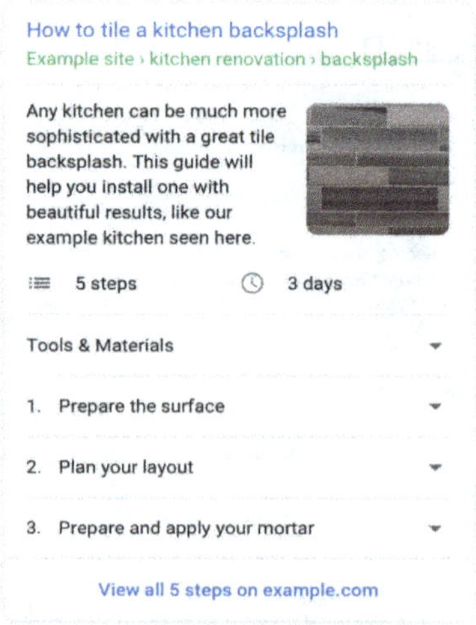

Source: Google, Voice Assisted Search, How To Example[64]
Say OK Google - Talk to Discovered Book – How To's

Each Schema type or class has dozens of properties specific to that Schema type. It is important to be familiar with which Schema type makes the most sense for your brand and how to best leverage its properties. It's important to choose the right class and complete the correct properties to prevent errors and warnings from Google. Schema.org doesn't give you any feedback on whether or not you have Schema set up properly or not. You will most likely rely on Google to guide you on what is correct and what needs to be corrected. Visit Discoveredbook.com/ Book to see the latest list of Google free tools and other Schema solutions that we recommend[65].

The power of Schema doesn't come from just being able to provide Structured Data or Rich Snippets, which are the same thing.

Structured Data means the data that is associated with an object.

Here are a couple of examples of structured data:

- Product - Title, description, part number, price, specs, availability
- Recipes - Calories, time to cook
- Events - Location, event time, venue, seats

Each Schema class has relevant properties, which is additional data (structured data or rich snippets) that helps us better understand that specific event, product, recipes, etc.

---

[65] *Say OK Google - Talk to Discovered Book – Schema Resources*

Logos and Social Badges

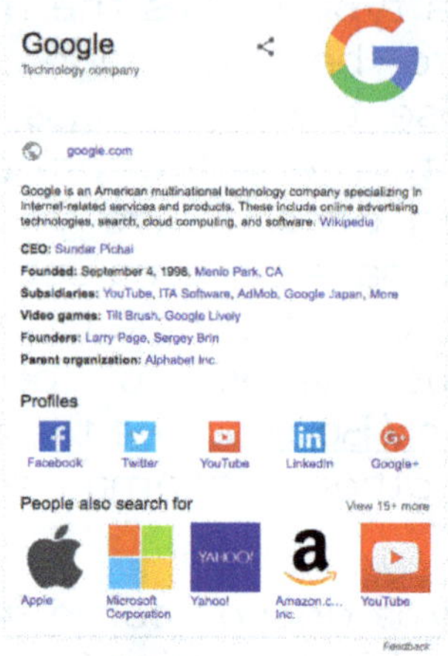

Source: Google, Logos and Social[66]

Say OK Google - Talk to Discovered Book - Logos and Social

Knowledge Panel (Knowledge Graph)

You may have seen the Knowledge Graph in action on the first page of Google search results.

This often comes in several shapes and forms. One example is the Knowledge Panel, which you can see in the image below:

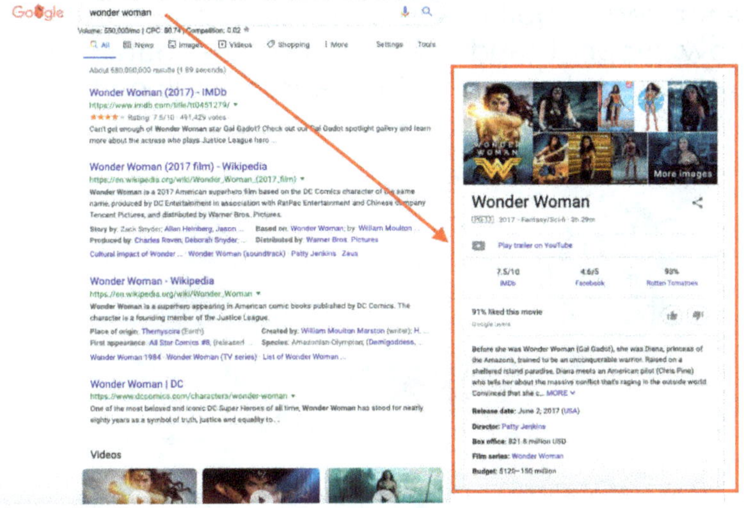

Source: Google, Knowledge Panel[67]

Say OK Google - Talk to Discovered Book – Knowledge Panel

Example of a Knowledge Panel, which is the information from Google's Knowledge Graph. The Knowledge Graph is extremely important as it enables Google to offer better search results to users.

In addition, the Knowledge Panel is becoming the backbone for voice search. That is because the Google Assistant, in many cases provides answer that comes from the Knowledge Graph, if one is available.

Building a Knowledge Panel for your brand must be on your radar as search engines, like Google have become Semantic, and they look for information provided in a Knowledge Graph format. We are seeing more and more reliance on this powerful little window.

Google started to build its Knowledge Graph back in 2012, and now your brand can contribute data to your Knowledge Graph, and enable search engines to access them in a format called Linked Open Data.

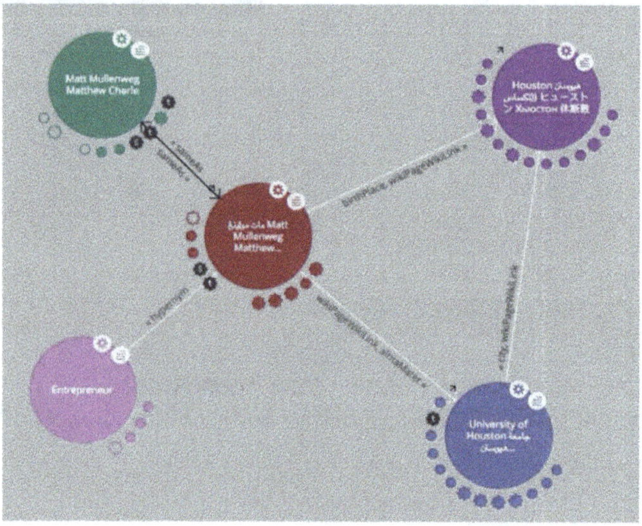

Source: LOD-Live, Linked Open Data[68]

Say OK Google - Talk to Discovered Book – Linked Open Data

Indeed, this format enables search engines to see your graph and extract relevant information from it to show it to users on the search results pages.

From these data points, we are helping the search engines build connections and relationships. Similar to the 6 degrees of Kevin Bacon. Who knew Kevin Bacon was connected to everyone in Hollywood. No one. Until someone built those connections for us.

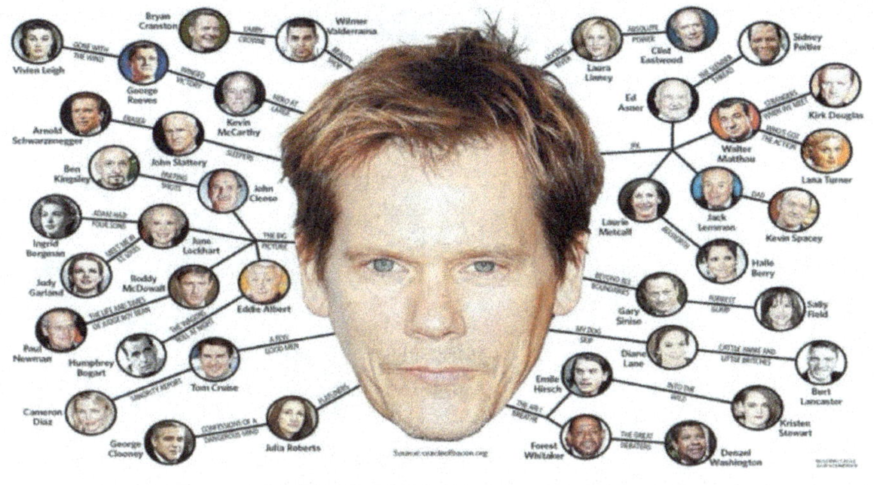

Source: Mark Robinson Writes, 6 Degrees of Kevin Bacon [69]
Say OK Google - Talk to Discovered Book – Kevin Bacon

When done well, we build a vocabulary of semantic data that can provide the Knowledge Graph, the Internet, and users the information that gives powerful meaning to our content and our brand.

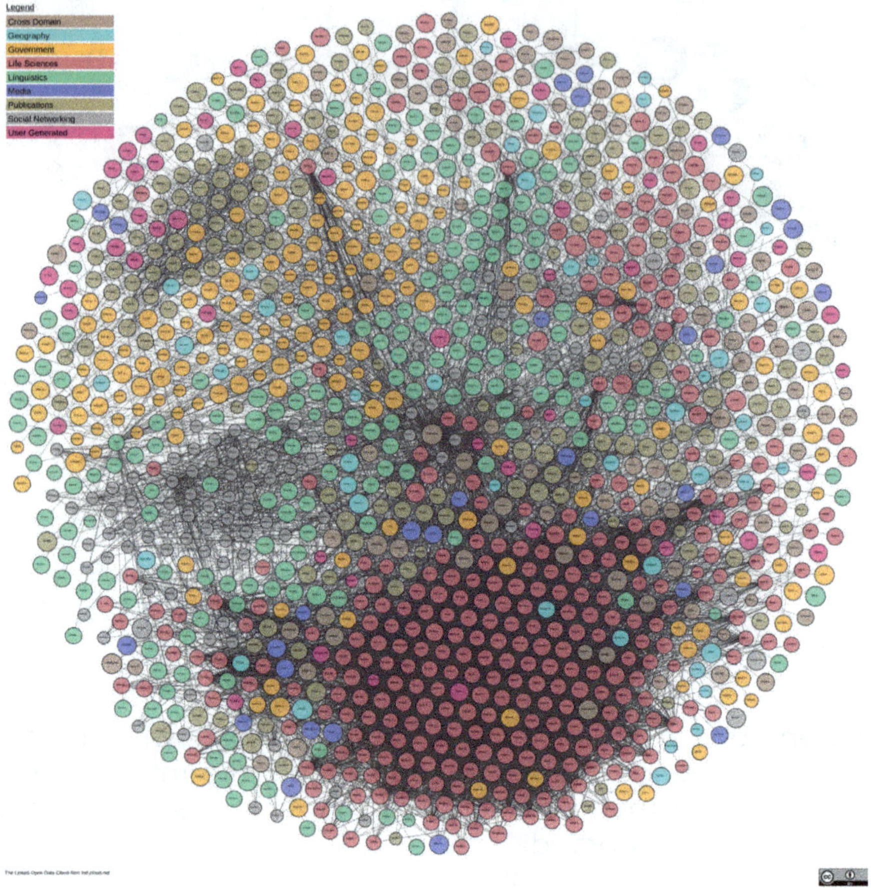

Source: Linked Open Data Cloud from LOD-Cloud.net [70]
Say OK Google - Talk to Discovered Book – LOD Cloud

This image is super hard to see in the book but the lower red portion of the cloud formation has a darker background color because it is heavily connected to the other data points of connection. To fully understand this, visit the site to see the interactive experience where you can see the connections between these different points. Super cool stuff, man!

We use a software called WordLift to help us with this process for our clients. WordLift is a Software-as-a-Service (SaaS) based solution that leverages on machine learning to elevate your SEO and your Expertise, Authority, and Trustworthiness (EAT)[71]. This process is easier with help from people that really get it. If you decide WordLift is a good fit, get the 10% coupon before you check out.

To learn more about this, you can read WordLift's Semantic SEO Guide to learn about how to integrate semantic meaning into your SEO Strategy[72]. Their site is filled with information to help you wrap your head around how all this works together.

"Twenty years after I am witnessing again to a similar – if not even more radical – transformation of our society as we race for the so-called AI transformation. This basically means applying machine learning, ontologies and knowledge graphs to optimize every process of our daily lives."

\- Andrea Volpini, CEO of WordLift

The WordLift team is amazing to work with and based on what is in the product roadmap, they are primed to lead SEO automation in the semantic and voice search realm. WordLift fits all sizes of brands, from Wordpress sites to large enterprise 20,000 pages sites.

---

71 *Say OK Google - Talk to Discovered Book - WordLift*

72 *Say OK Google - Talk to Discovered Book - WordLift Guide*

When you provide additional information about your content and what it stands for, then the engines understand who to send to your site to send more of the right people. More organic traffic from people with the intent to pay to solve their problem equals jackpot!

Wanna Pass on Schema?

You might be thinking "I'm not doing Schema today and I get plenty of website traffic so I don't need to do it."

We typically see one of two things. Brands that think they are doing the right thing with Schema or brands that are doing nothing but SEO and ads. We only have so much time in the day and you can't be expected to know everything. But unfortunately, you don't know what you don't know. Schema.org and Google Developer tools themselves both tell you *exactly* what to do for each Schema class (or type) and its properties.

Some may argue, "at least we're doing something!" An improperly implemented Schema strategy can be better than nothing but not if you forget a required property (structured data field). That results in errors that cause your pages to not appear as high in search results. We often won't see the results that we want.

How Does Schema Work Exactly?

Here's where it gets fun. Schema is technical. We often find SEO agencies and ad agencies don't play in the Schema sandbox with us. Schema is created with a programming language called JSON-LD.

JSON is not hard to understand for techies, but if you're not technical, it's a foreign language, literally. Because it's programming, it's not fun for most people, which is why I assume most agencies haven't embraced it fully yet.

Schema can be applied directly to your webpages, on the website layer. Or with programs like Google Tag Manager. Schema is applied on an invisible layer between your website and the discovery engines. Everything on the web is in the cloud. Most people have a hard time wrapping their head around the cloud. The cloud *does* exist in our physical world. We just don't see it. I often refer to the cloud as the world's biggest computer. It is unimaginable to think of how big that is but it pretty incredible.

When it comes to how Schema actually works, I want you to imagine that you're going to see a play. You have incredible seats, right behind the orchestra pit. You can see the conductor and the tops of some of the instruments and the stage are perfectly positioned right in front of you. As you examine the theatre, you see this huge red curtain that is shielding you from everything and everyone that is busily scrambling behind the curtain to put the last-minute touches on the set or the stage.

The house lights start dim as the last few people (which would totally be me) are shuffling to their seats. The orchestra starts to play their music and the house lights go down. The curtain opens and you see this vibrant set filled with beautiful vivid colors. Professional actors walk on stage, surrounded by meticulously crafted props. As the star of the show gracefully glides on stage, you are in awe of the sounds of the orchestra, the beautiful ballad, and you melt into a world of wonder and imagination. As you watch this performance, the people on stage are the only people you are meant to see.

For that show to run smoothly, there are dozens of people who you are never supposed to see:

- There are people running lights.
- There are people running the sound system.
- There is someone in the back, shuffling people in and out of wardrobe changes.
- There is someone on stage left and someone else on

stage right with the script, making sure that the right people are going on stage at the right moment.
- There are people moving props on and off the stage every time the curtain closes.

All of these people, behind the curtain and behind the stage, are a huge part of what makes the show so incredible. It's not just the actors. The actors alone wouldn't be a show. The actors without music wouldn't be a show. The actors without wardrobe and makeup and hair wouldn't be a show. Everyone else turns the show into an extraordinary, memorable experience.

Now, let's frame the performance into terms relevant to the search. Here are the players in the performance of the search:

The Stage

Page 1 of Google Search results. The stage is the answer that you get through online or voice search. The stage is the results you get when you ask your phone a question on voice or type it into a search window. The stage is what you see or hear as the answer.

The Actors

This is your content, your website pages, your social media. These are the characters of your brand. The voice of your brand. The mission, purpose, and value of your brand.

The Curtain

This is the layer between your webpages and Schema. This is Google Tag Manager.

The Real Stars of the Show

This is everyone behind the curtain that makes the show remarkable. This is Schema.

That Annoying Guy

The guy in the aisle selling wine and snacks at the precise time that no one wants to look away from the stage. Those are ads.

Schema done well turns an ordinary show into a **Tony-nominated performance.**

Schema gives your content meaning (through additional structured data) and creates a visually rich preview of shoppers.

Remember when we talked about our imaginary weekend where AMC saved the well-being of the kids (and me)? The example that I gave you with the movies and engaging results, including movie thumbnail images, cast member pictures, showtimes, reviews, a map, phone number, and all that fun stuff? That is a Schema-optimized experience that the AMC brand owns, which influences the shopper's behavior (in this case, my family).

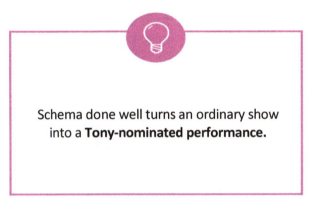

Here's another secret about Schema. Schema gives you the opportunity to serve rich and engaging content that is highly valuable and relevant to the right people. Let's say you've stepped up your Schema game, and your site has organically ranked for the right intent with the right content. Schema supercharges your content to become a visually engaging experience right there on the first page of Google. Just like my desperate search for movie showtimes, you can give your consumers more information than they realize they need to decide, organically and visually, on page one of Google without being overly promotional or sales-y. It is a naturally delightful experience for new consumers discovering your brand or existing customers to be reminded about your brand's value again.

Shoppers not only expect brands to keep them engaged with personalized experiences, but they also expect those experiences to be beautiful, visually styled experiences. Thanks, Instagram and Pinterest! And in the past, page one of Google hasn't exactly been visually tantalizing. Schema gives you the opportunity to change that with a rich visual preview of your content to connect your consumer to the content that you have already created for them.

How awesome is that? All of the amazing images that you have within the copy of the page can now be seen in a little thumbnail image and previews within the organic search results on page one of Google?! Mic drop.

Common Schema Mistakes

As mentioned, not everyone uses Schema well. Here are some of the most common mistakes that we see when it comes to Schema.

Mistake #1 - You Think You are Already Doing Schema

The most common mistake we see is "I am totally doing Schema right." Remember less than .3% were actually doing Schema right[36].

Rich snippets are most commonly what people confuse Schema with. A rich snippet is rich content that is a visually engaging preview of your brand provides. But rich snippets alone are not enough. Engaging, contextualized content is what Google wants more of but rich snippets alone are not enough. Think of it this way, it's like making a peanut butter and jelly sandwich without the bread. Or getting all of the fixings without the burger.

Who wants that? No one.

You could be missing out on some of the most powerful benefits of Schema without realizing it. Maybe your agency is doing what they do best and didn't know about Schema either. This is pretty typical since Schema is a bit technical. It's not our fault. We only have so much time in the day and it's hard to keep up with everything that Google expects from your website and content.

Mistake #2 - Content Doesn't Match Schema

The structured data doesn't match the content on the page. Schema offers more than 830+ classes (or types), as we discussed, so any normal technologist or marketer would be like a kid in a candy shop.

There are so many possibilities!

Sometimes our imagination (or interpretation) of our web pages and content can get the best of us. We get excited and we tell Schema we have a lot of awesomeness on our pages that might not actually be there.

My first car was a Toyota Tercel. And I could choose between AC or automatic transmission. I opted for AC and chose the manual transmission (or a stick). I am a dinosaur, so I learned how to drive cars on a stick (most kids today would say, What's a stick?"). "

Technically, I could associate my entry level four-speed Toyota with other cars that also have manual transmissions, like Ferraris and Lamborghinis! We all have manual transmissions, right? Riiiiiight.

I will just tell Schema that my car is an Italian performance car. Google thinks I am a Ferrari and tells the world I am a Ferrari, and when they send people to my website and see that I am pretty much the cheapest Toyota you can buy... let's just say Google doesn't like that.

Your site can get penalized if you pretend to have something other than what is actually on your page.

The moral of the story is: Your Schema Markup data should match the content that actually exists on the page.

Mistake #3-Ignoring Google's guidelines

No one loves rules. But Google's guidelines for Schema are very clear and easy to follow but some may like to ignore them completely.

Here's an example we see all the time when an organization uses the Organization Schema of every single web page.

When you tell Schema about your product, that is the Product Schema type.

Well, which is it?

An organization or a product? Seems simple but we see this over and over again. It's like everyone read that same blog that probably thought they had Schema properly set up too.

Mistake #4 - You don't optimize

Have you heard the phrase: If you don't grow, you die? Like a plant without water. I have a better one for you.

> If your brand doesn't **optimize, evolve, and adapt**, you will lose.

One and done is not a thing in our world. No matter how much you think you might be killing it online, remember this, **you can ALWAYS do better** ... or someone else can.

Here's an example of when and how this commonly happens.

You set up a page for Schema Markup. It looks great.

The pages get tons of organic traffic, tons of engagement, AND tons of comments. You are the queen (or king) in your office. After you award yourself the President of the Pat-Yourself-on-the-Back Club, you get busy. You don't check on your pages for a while, which turns into months. Before you know it, all of those awesome comments are slowing the page down and Google doesn't like slow, so Schema stops working. And you, the President of the club, didn't even realize it.

If you just optimized... this all could have been avoided.

Other Schema Considerations

Here are just a couple of things to ponder as you start to wrap your brain around ways you can use Schema:

- What does your brand stand for?
- What is your brand's purpose?
- What makes your brand unique?
- What are your competitive differentiators?
- What is your brand's voice? Persona? Traits?
- What is the purpose of your website, content, brand, and your products?
- Do any of these answers appear when you Google your brand name, the problem you solve, or the consumer intent you know your brand can fulfill?

Every discovery engine and every voice engine will hear, see, and feel the heart and soul of your brand. For maybe the first time ever, people will understand why they should buy your product. In a world that is so loud and noisy and distracted, your brand is the one that stands out.

I'm sure your head is starting to spin as you process and absorb this. You're going to imagine thousands of ways you can apply this. Please understand that Schema is a game-changer for your brand. Unless you are in the entertainment industry, I am almost willing to bet that you can be a pioneer in doing Schema properly for your industry or product category.

ASSISTED SEARCH

When researching anything, people can spend hours and even days trying to satisfy their research curiosity. Sometimes, I lose track of time and don't even realize what I started to search for in the first place. Those days, I feel really old and absent-minded.

The customer journey is not linear. Here are a few key moments that are important for you to understand during the journey for the consumer.

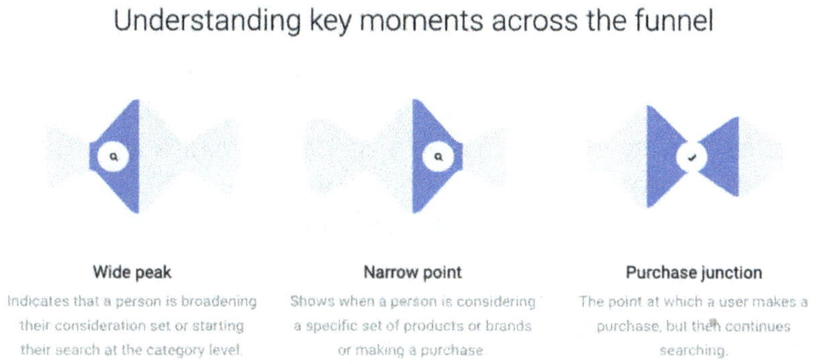

Understanding key moments across the funnel
Wide peak
Indicates that a person is broadening their consideration set or starting their search at the category level.
Narrow point
Shows when a person is considering a specific set of products or brands or making a purchase.
Purchase junction
The point at which a user makes a purchase, but then continues searching.

Source: Think by Google[75]

Say OK Google - Talk to Discovered Book – Path to Purchase

<u>Wide Peak</u>

This is when a person is broadening their consideration set or starting their search at the category level. An example would be I know I want to plan the trip of a lifetime, a bucket list trip but I am torn between a few destinations. I start my discovery with a wide broad approach to learn more about the areas. I narrow it down

Tahiti because I am 100% certain that is where I want to go.

Narrow Point

This is when a person is considering a specific set of products or brands and they are close to deciding who they are going to make a purchase with. Consider another travel example: Perhaps I am deciding between a cruise through Tahiti like Paul Gauguin Cruises OR an island stay at The St. Regis. At this point, I have narrowed in on a couple of brands that I'm torn between but I am super close to deciding based on what I find out about the brands.

Purchase Junction

This is where it gets really interesting: The purchase junction technically is the point where I make a purchase. I personally decide on Paul Gauguin Cruises because I can travel around to multiple French Polynesian Islands on an exquisite luxury ship, opposed to being stuck at one resort our entire vacation. And at this point you would think that I would be done searching, and that my research is over. But what actually happens is I continue to search. You might be scratching your head thinking we're done, we won. But think about it for yourself when you plan a trip. The accommodations are just one piece of the puzzle. Now that I know that I am taking a Paul Gauguin Cruise to cruise around the French Polynesian islands, I actually have to plan my excursions, where I'm eating, or how I'm getting there.

I'm sure you've heard of the term omnichannel, multi-device, multi-platform, or multi-modal. All of these terms represent the state of how consumers search and buy today. Google has a website called Think with Google. They provide insight based on years of search and behavioral data. You can sign up for weekly thought starters if that insight adds value to your world.

Think with Google is a treasure trove of valuable insight of what Google has learned about search behavior, consumer behavior, buying behavior, and sometimes even by industry, by sector, or by vertical. It provides genuinely useful insight, in easy-to-digest, bite-size pieces regarding how consumers behave in relation to searching across multiple platforms, across multiple devices, in some cases, until they buy.

Google provide trends and summaries on busy search or shopping times, like shopper search and buying behavior during the holiday season, for example, Black Friday 2018, to help brands understand what behavior they tracked the week prior, which started the busiest buying time for many consumer brands. They broke the buyers up into three or four different categories, and told you the consumers' spending behaviors related to each category, depending on your product category fit for that specific consumer buying cycle. Essentially, they explained that "this is the search and shopping behavior we saw and how you can capitalize on it for your brand through the weeks leading up to Christmas and a few weeks beyond."

To be able to see stats on Black Friday/ Cyber Monday literally the week after it happened is incredibly valuable to an agile brand that can respond quickly to consumer market changes. You can quickly understand where you need to pivot just a little bit if or when you do not capture the buyers that you thought were in your brand category. Google even went so far as to explain what happens after the Christmas holiday. If you sell gift cards or if you have a brick-and-mortar location, for instance, these are things that you want to do after the holiday to ensure that the sales continue to ride that holiday buying wave. Now, Google wants you to buy ads but the insights are free and relevant to anyone selling products to people.

There are several featured insights on Think by Google right now that have a very similar theme. The theme is about the customer buying journey and how the buying journey is not linear at all. They give many different actual user case studies of all of their searching and buying touch points.

We mustn't forget that consumers are research obsessed. They look for something better with greater value partially because of how we've conditioned them to always look for something better. Consumers look for something better even if they enjoyed the product they used, which means consumers today, have very little brand product loyalty.

One example that they gave was for a woman who was planning a trip. Her trip research started on her desktop with four different search queries. She started to look at destinations, then she narrowed the destinations down. She started to look for hotel accommodations, then she narrowed the hotels down. Over this period of these search queries, she had more than 100 touchpoints. Later, she started her research process back up on her mobile device, where she continued travel planning for several weeks. In just this one customer example, there were more than 400 touchpoints in her buying journey. 400!

There's a good news-bad news scenario playing out. The good news is we literally have hundreds of opportunities to influence their path to purchase, thanks to their obsession with research, reviews, and social proof. The bad news is we literally have hundreds of touchpoints across devices to make sure we are being found for.

A male consumer, shopping for a video game, had the highest number of touchpoints (more than 500). Consumers searching for fairly simple products, like books or razors, still had 100+ touchpoints before their final trip store to buy. Check out Google's site to see the super cool interactive shopper journeys.[76]

---

[76] *Say OK Google - Talk to Discovered Book - Shopper Journeys*

Searching for Innovation

Let's talk about how you can assist the buyer in their search journey. When I think of assisted search similar to the zero moments of truth we talked about with Google where the buyer has decided, before getting to a search box, to buy something or to inquire or discover a product or service.

When we recognize that the consumer has so many touchpoints, in so many different places on so many different channels spanning multiple devices and mediums, how can we use this to make that journey better? This is not about being found on every single channel. It's understanding what channel we need to be found on at that precise moment.

In Google, this is called micro-moments. If you run Google ads, you're probably familiar with micro-moments. Micro-moments are these moments in time where a person tries to fulfil intent to understand "how to" do something or "where to find" something. If you can be found in that micro-moment, with the best relevant content that moves them forward in their journey, then you can potentially influence the consumer towards your product.

It's tough to create content not knowing:

- If it is what people want;
- Is it engaging enough that they will trust and buy our products?
- Is this content worthy enough to share?

The opportunity assisted search gives you starts with a deeper understanding into what consumers need to see and at what point in the journey they need to see it and how to get that content in front of them.

Brands must understand:

- What questions will they ask?
- What intent are they trying to fulfill?
- Are they even aware they have a problem at all?
- What solutions are they trying to find?
- Are they looking for a video, FAQs, or a review?

You can deliver content to handle each one of these issues through an assisted buying experience.

One cool option is to be there through one of the voice assistants like Siri, OK Google, Cortana, or Alexa. Even better, you can create your own assisted persona artificial intelligent assistant that is not only helping consumers in their buying journey but is also learning. Each interaction with a person teaches your assistant what preferences people have, and what experiences, questions, or interactions help results in more sales!

This is something happening right now with dozens of brands. It is innovative. It is emerging and, in some industries, has not yet been proven, other than with the proof of sales, which is pretty strong proof if you ask me. We'll talk more about this when we explore voice later in the book.

Shifting from keywords to speakable

One of the things, I am really excited about is being able to move from keywords into speakable, natural language. When I say speakable, think about natural conversational language that you have with friends, family, and coworkers.

Begin to shift your thinking to those intent-focused questions because as we start to rely more on hands-free and less on links, this will be a lesson worth learning early and keeping top of mind.

Consider all of your old content that may be instructional or informative. Those lengthy 2,000-word pages that your team worked on tirelessly, which hopefully resulted in pretty decent brand awareness and engagement. Repurpose what you have that is good and optimize it for speakable, natural language and semantic (what's the real meaning) searches.

When Adobe surveyed 1,500 consumers about their brand experience here are some of the common themes they uncovered:

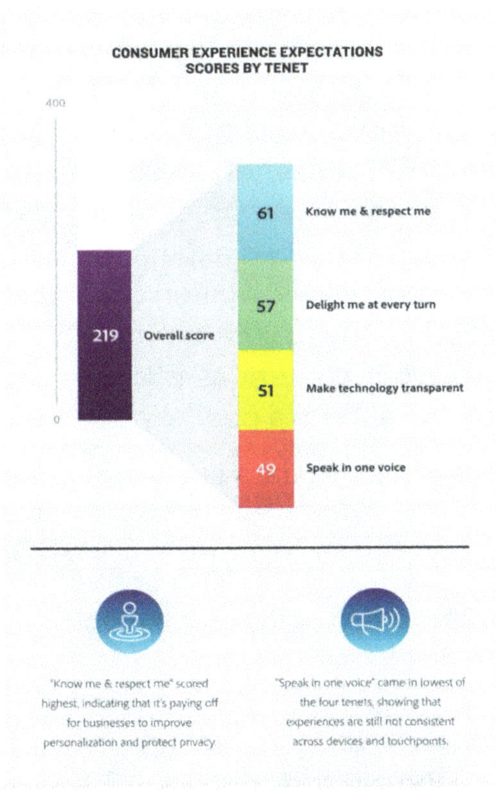

Source: Adobe Consumer Expectations Survey 2018[77]

Say OK Google - Talk to Discovered Book - Customer Experience Adobe

- **Know and respect me.** The consumer most valued being treated personally and with great regard. This suggests that brands recent focus on improving personalization and recognizing privacy choices are really starting to payoff.

- **Try to delight me at every turn.** This underscores how marketers have to operationalize going above and beyond at every touchpoint of the customer's experience.
- **Make technology transparent.** Be upfront if customers are talking to a robot during a chat session. Let them know so they realize they're not having a conversation with a person.

- **Speak in one voice.** If you can make the experience better, make their lives easier, with less frustration, across devices, over multiple touchpoints, then do that. But don't introduce areas of frustration or friction that make the experience worse. Nearly half of people said that if they have a bad experience with the brand online, they most likely wouldn't buy that brand. It's hard to get someone to click on your link to visit your page to view your content as it is. The last thing you want to do is give them a poor experience.

What's interesting about some of this data is everyone, no matter their gender or their age, wants businesses to give them personalized service. EVERYONE. Future focused brands are optimizing their older, high ranking content so that it can be easily discovered through a conversational search and discovery queries.

Another way to look at a voice assisted search is by understanding the emotional stress the buying decision has on your consumer. Choosing a doctor versus a makeup is a very different level of stress. By understanding how you can reduce their stress and their friction during their buying journey, you can provide great utility and assistance with the best content. If you know where is there going to be an objection, what issues you're going to have to overcome every single time for them to make a decision, then how can you integrate that during their touchpoints? Can you help educate them and influence them to make the right decision? You absolutely can.

Here are some of your considerations:

- How can you assist?
- Where do you assist?
- What is the best way to deliver that experience?

Accessibility

Accessibility is something we often don't spend a lot of time thinking about. Just to put things in perspective, most of us have had access to the internet for decades. In that time, you have probably discovered endless amounts of data, experiences, videos, and teaching.

Imagine for a moment that you are one of the 8 million people in the United States who is blind[78]. And voice doesn't exist on the internet in a rich and engaging experience. For years, we hear coworkers, friends, and family members talk about things that they saw on the internet, on Facebook, Instagram, LinkedIn, and so on. But you can't see it. Not only can you not see it, but many websites don't have an audio translation for what seeing people can experience through the site.

---

[78] Say OK Google - Talk to Discovered Book – *Visually Impaired Stats*

You have an opportunity as a brand to give everyone, impaired or not, a delightful experience.

This shouldn't be something that you do to meet ADA compliance regulations or requirements. This should be something you do for humankind so everyone has the ability to search, discover, and understand your brand.

Back in the day, ADA compliance on a website meant that you had to have three sizes of fonts: small, medium, and large. This would show up as a little A, a bigger A, and a big, big, big A. That was it. Who does that serve? It serves visually impaired people who can see but just need larger letters. It does not people who are visually challenged.

Imagine how podcasts, audio books, and Audible have changed the dynamic to include people through sound. Voice will give your brand an opportunity to engage and delight millions of people who, right now, can't see or hear your website. That, in itself, is enough to be super excited about how the consumer experience is changing and the opportunity for all people to create a connection with your brand.

For more information on making your websites accessible, see the Resources chapter at the end of this book.

Assisting after the buying journey

Another thing that's important to understand is that the journey doesn't stop at the purchase. Often, we will do everything we can to get someone to buy but we miss an opportunity to nurture that person into a lifelong customer. Yes, I am saying your job is not done after the purchase, rather it continues until the customer becomes an advocate for your brand. At that point, there should be someone responsible for maintaining, fostering, nurturing, and supporting your community of advocates. They are worth their weight in gold and will be a tremendous asset to your brand. If you struggle with brand loyalty, this is one potential solution.

This presents a unique opportunity for brands. A friend of mine, Greg A. Sausaman, is the author of a book called "Inside the Box, The Power of Complementary Branding." He is an expert in complementary branding. Complementary branding means you can provide complementary added value services for your customers. And this may not be a fit for all brands, but it will be a fit for some.

Is there a way that you can add more value to your customers' experience at the same time making your product experience better as well?

This could also be another channel of revenue for your brand. His book is a great read, and can be purchased Amazon[79].

Going back to the Tahiti example, if I provide accommodations, surely can assist with some of the research that my consumer is doing after they book with my location, whether that's excursions, meals, transportation, or travel insurance. There's is a way to make our consumers' lives easier and more delightful beyond the purchase.

Look at the customer discovery experience through the lens of the consumer, with an intimate level of detail

---

[79] Say OK Google - Talk to Discovered Book – *Inside the Box*

about their intent combined with the experiences that consumers expect and desire from your brand.

Creating new experiences and ways to engage with your consumer from discovery to beyond the purchase can be tackled bit by bit. And don't forget that you should always optimize and discover ways to improve the process and experience for your consumers.

SEARCH TAKEAWAYS

Author and motivational speaker Simon Sinek spoke at John Maxwell's Live2Lead leadership development program in 2016. In his 30-minute talk, he addressed how leaders have created an environment fueled by competition[80]. We've become conditioned to measure success in numbers only. We've done that because business has demanded that of us. We have to understand that the environment that we created often doesn't allow failure. It often doesn't provide the training, knowledge, and resources that people need to succeed, yet, we expect them to deliver at a higher level than, quite frankly, they're equipped to handle.

As you look at whether or not you're doing Schema or assisted search or other technologies, understand that most of us have not been given the support that we need to do our jobs to the best of our ability. This is not a personal reflection on you or I. It is the nature of most business environments. As leaders, we choose how we lead and we choose how we support our team, which is what our job should really be about. However, these things are not widely understood. They are not backed by hundreds of case studies that will minimize your risk down to zero. You aren't going to see thousands of examples of where it's done right.

I hope you're going into this with an open mind, accepting that your team might not know and that's okay. The best you can do is understand that you need to start doing something now and how can you fail faster?

---

[80] Say OK Google - Talk to Discovered Book – *Simon Sinek*

Key Takeaways

- Understand consumer intent
- Validate the journey annually
- Know your current position on search
- Implement Schema (the right way)
- Always be experimenting and optimizing when it comes to customer experience

SECTION 2: VOICE

IMAGINE A WORLD

Imagine you are working late in the office. At 5:45 p.m., you realize that family dinner is your responsibility tonight and you completely dropped the ball. You instantly imagine a dramatization of your kids wreaking havoc and mayhem on your perfect, neatly stocked pantry, eating every sugary snack that you have. They are hungry and there is no one there to ~~guide~~ force them to make healthier choices.

With one broad sweep of your arm, you manage to shove everything that you were working on in your laptop bag and you are downstairs in the car in a few Olympic-gold-medal, sprinter-worthy moments.

As you leave, you tell your voice assistant to get you home fast. She pulls up your home address in your Google Maps app as you mumble a silent prayer that everyone else decided to leave work early today so that the highway isn't its usual gridlocked mess.

Like a scene out of the movie "Office Space," you frantically switch from lane to lane in an attempt to make it home faster just so you can feel like you are not failing as a parent.

While you're in this panic, something strange is happening. After your voice assistant told you the best route to get you home, she is busy doing something else, too. Based on what your voice assistant has learned about you, she realizes something is different. Your behavior over time has taught her that you typically arrive home well before 6 p.m. and you're normally ordering food or going to your favorite local restaurant for happy hour (for food, not drinks!).

You hear your completely calm, friendly voice assistant say, "You will arrive home in 47 minutes. Would you like me to have dinner delivered to your home? I can pick up Chipotle for Ellie and sushi for Damon and have dinner delivered by 6:20 p.m."

With a huge sigh of relief and an immediate burden lifted from your shoulders, you calmly replied, "Yes." The sense of urgency is gone and you can arrive home in one relatively calm piece.

The feeling of panic has left your body and you can take a deep breath.

This may seem like a far-off futuristic scenario, but it isn't.

Our phones are tracking everything we are doing right now, whether it's Alexa, Siri, Google, or the apps that help us make our lives better. Our life experiences are personalized with every swipe, tap, text, and search.

In addition to simplifying our personal lives, voice experiences allow us to learn more about our shoppers and how to create better, more personalized experiences for them.

Voice can help us learn about:

- What you like and dislike;
- What meals you've eaten;
- Which credit cards you prefer to use;
- Everywhere you drive and frequent;
- Where you live, work, and play;
- Your habits and preferences.

Your voice assistant has its own unique algorithm just for you. Your personal algorithm is customized with your name, your life, and your preferences written all over it.

It may seem Big Brother-ish but it's really not. In fact, this level of personalization is what consumers are beginning to demand from our brands. Every interaction with a consumer is another piece of the puzzle that tells us more about how they wish to have conversations and connections with your brands.

The challenge is that we often don't know how to find these interactions or what to do with them. And that is completely normal. The human brain can only process so much information (literally three things) before we just go into overload.

A voice assistant built on machine learning with the processing speed to handle the entire internet, now that's a totally different story.

VOICE OPPORTUNITY

"The future is already here - it's just not evenly distributed."

– William Gibson

Before we get too deep into voice, I have to give a huge shout out to the team at Voicebot.ai. It is exciting to learn about voice but challenging to find reliable data, Voicebot.ai makes that possible and is cited many times in this book. The data is their blood, sweat and tears and I am grateful to their team. Voicebot produces the leading independent research, online publication, newsletter and podcast focused on the voice and AI industries. Thousands of entrepreneurs, developers, investors, analysts and other industry leaders look to Voicebot each week for the latest news, data, analysis and insights defining the trajectory of the next great computing platform. At Voicebot, we give voice to a revolution. To be the first in the know on the latest in the voice industry, consider joining their Insider subscription, which is very reasonably priced, less than a meal. Please check them out so you can learn too[84].

Now let's get to the fun stuff! Voice advancements in the last 20 years have been incredible, which means the opportunities are endless! The first voice (or speech) recognition software was created in 1961 by IBM.

---

[84] *Say OK Google - Talk to Discovered Book – Voicebot*

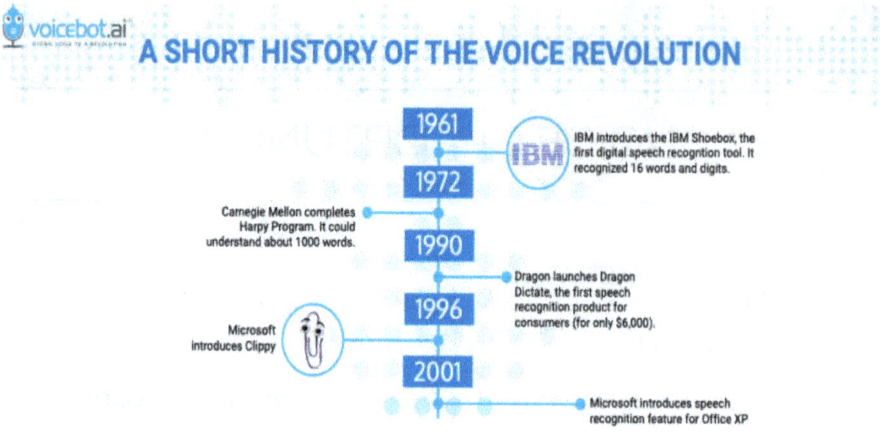

Source: Voicebot.ai[85]

Say OK Google - Talk to Discovered Book - Voice Assistant Timeline

The voice world stays quiet for 10 years until 2011, when Apple releases Siri, in classic Apple style.

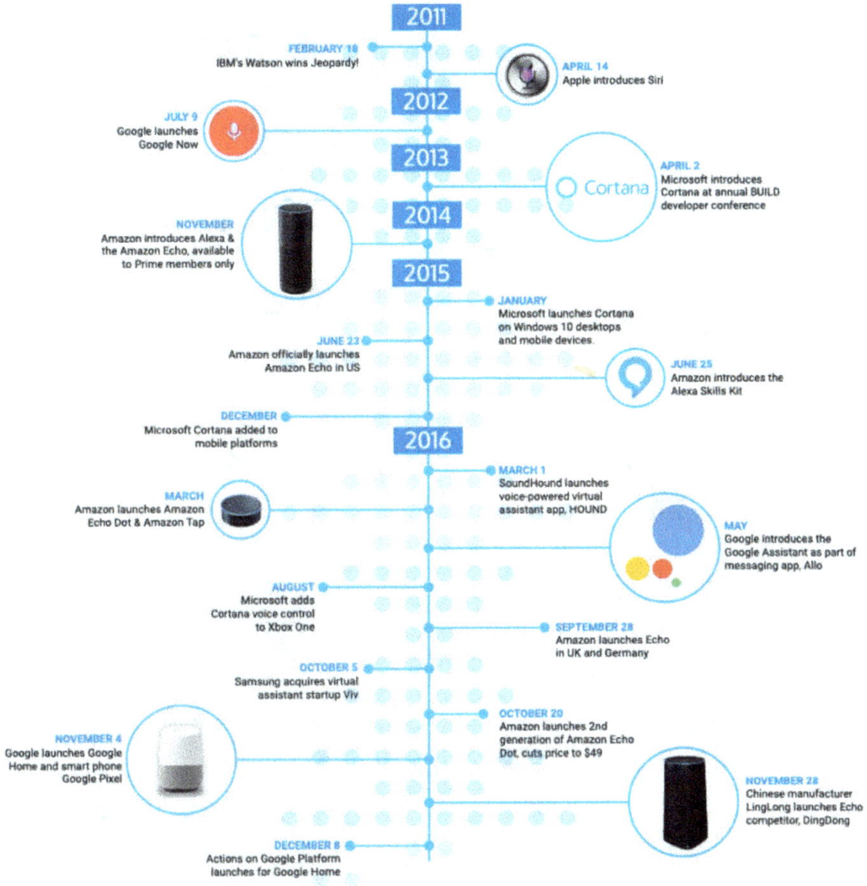

2011
FEBRUARY 16
IBM's Watson wins Jeopardy!
APRIL 14
Apple introduces Siri
2012
JULY 9
Google launches Google Now
2013
Cortana
APRIL 2
Microsoft introduces Cortana at annual BUILD developer conference
2014
NOVEMBER
Amazon introduces Alexa & the Amazon Echo, available to Prime members only
2015
JANUARY
Microsoft launches Cortana on Windows 10 desktops and mobile devices.
JUNE 23
Amazon officially launches Amazon Echo in US
JUNE 25
Amazon introduces the Alexa Skills Kit
DECEMBER
Microsoft Cortana added to mobile platforms
2016
MARCH 1
SoundHound launches voice-powered virtual assistant app, HOUND
MARCH
Amazon launches Amazon Echo Dot & Amazon Tap
MAY
Google introduces the Google Assistant as part of messaging app, Allo
AUGUST
Microsoft adds Cortana voice control to Xbox One
SEPTEMBER 28
Amazon launches Echo in UK and Germany
OCTOBER 5
Samsung acquires virtual assistant startup Viv
OCTOBER 20
Amazon launches 2nd generation of Amazon Echo Dot, cuts price to $49
NOVEMBER 4
Google launches Google Home and smart phone Google Pixel
NOVEMBER 28
Chinese manufacturer LingLong launches Echo competitor, DingDong
DECEMBER 8
Actions on Google Platform launches for Google Home

Source: Voicebot.ai[85]

Say OK Google - Talk to Discovered Book - Voice Assistant Timeline

The market still responds to Apple's bold voice move, with:

- 2011 Apple Siri is announced
- 2012 Google announces Google Now
- 2013 Microsoft announces Cortana
- 2014 Amazon introduces Alexa

From 2015 to today, voice has made incredible advances.

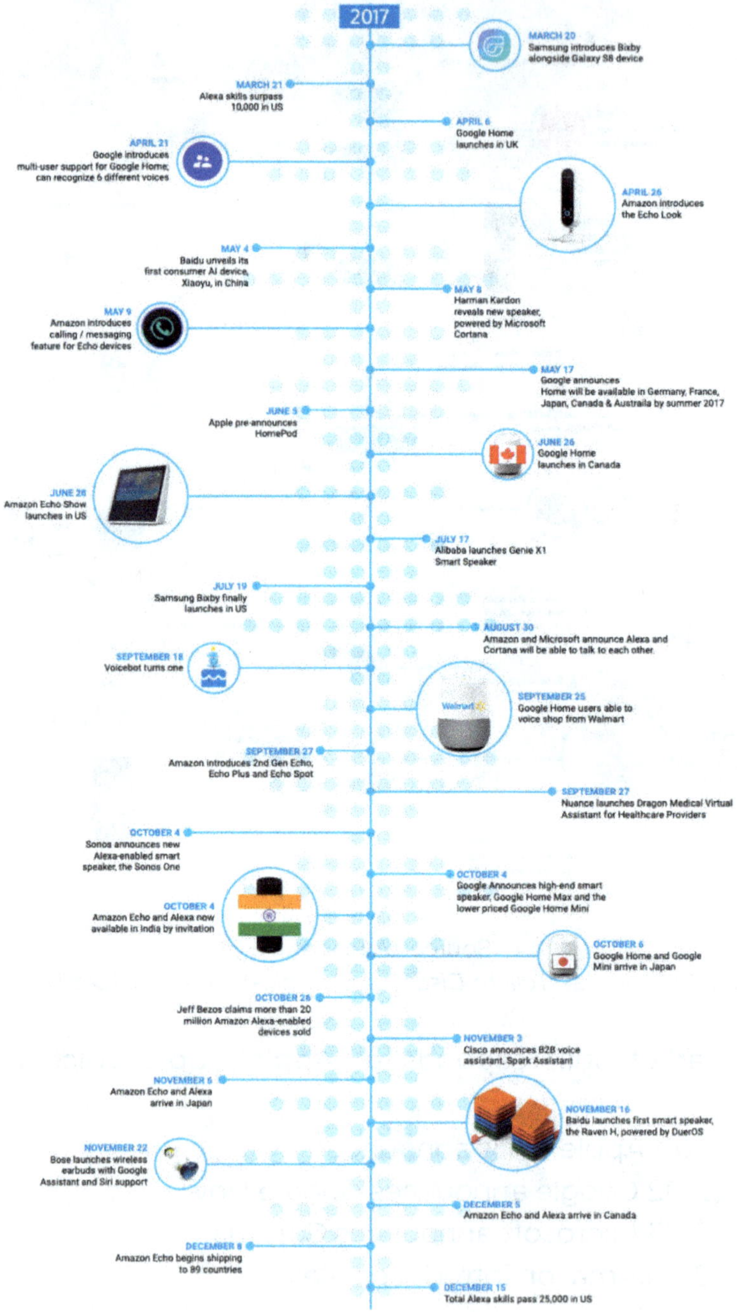

2017
MARCH 20
Samsung introduces Bixby alongside Galaxy S8 device
MARCH 21
Alexa skills surpass 10,000 in US
APRIL 6
Google Home launches in UK
APRIL 21
Google introduces multi-user support for Google Home; can recognize 6 different voices
APRIL 26
Amazon introduces the Echo Look
MAY 4
Baidu unveils its first consumer AI device, Xiaoyu, in China
MAY 8
Harman Kardon reveals new speaker, powered by Microsoft Cortana
MAY 9
Amazon introduces calling / messaging feature for Echo devices
MAY 17
Google announces Home will be available in Germany, France, Japan, Canada & Australia by summer 2017
JUNE 5
Apple pre-announces HomePod
JUNE 26
Google Home launches in Canada
JUNE 28
Amazon Echo Show launches in US
JULY 17
Alibaba launches Genie X1 Smart Speaker
JULY 19
Samsung Bixby finally launches in US
AUGUST 30
Amazon and Microsoft announce Alexa and Cortana will be able to talk to each other
SEPTEMBER 18
Voicebot turns one
SEPTEMBER 25
Google Home users able to voice shop from Walmart
SEPTEMBER 27
Amazon introduces 2nd Gen Echo, Echo Plus and Echo Spot
SEPTEMBER 27
Nuance launches Dragon Medical Virtual Assistant for Healthcare Providers
OCTOBER 4
Sonos announces new Alexa-enabled smart speaker, the Sonos One
OCTOBER 4
Google Announces high-end smart speaker, Google Home Max and the lower priced Google Home Mini
OCTOBER 4
Amazon Echo and Alexa now available in India by invitation
OCTOBER 6
Google Home and Google Mini arrive in Japan
OCTOBER 26
Jeff Bezos claims more than 20 million Amazon Alexa-enabled devices sold
NOVEMBER 3
Cisco announces B2B voice assistant, Spark Assistant
NOVEMBER 6
Amazon Echo and Alexa arrive in Japan
NOVEMBER 16
Baidu launches first smart speaker, the Raven H, powered by DuerOS
NOVEMBER 22
Bose launches wireless earbuds with Google Assistant and Siri support
DECEMBER 5
Amazon Echo and Alexa arrive in Canada
DECEMBER 8
Amazon Echo begins shipping to 89 countries
DECEMBER 15
Total Alexa skills pass 25,000 in US

Source: Voicebot.ai[85]

Say OK Google - Talk to Discovered Book - Voice Assistant Timeline

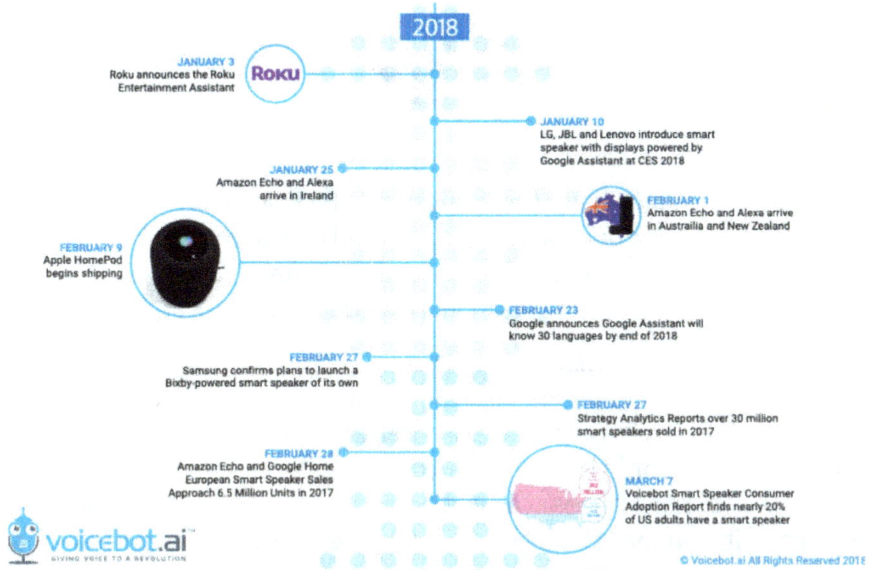

Source: Voicebot.ai[85]

Say OK Google - Talk to Discovered Book - Voice Assistant Timeline

The voice experience has improved so much that people actually want to talk to artificial people (robots, chatbots, and machines). Remember the days before texting when you have to pick up the phone? Even earlier, when would actually have to drive to someone's house, just to have a conversation? And if driving wasn't an option, you could always send a pigeon, telegram, or letter!

We can speak two to three times faster than we can type per minute. And that's based on a real keyboard, not just a five-inch phone screen keyboard. It completely makes sense that all of these big companies like Google, Amazon, Facebook, and Microsoft are investing so heavily in voice.

Voice is not the Innovation. The Innovation is our ability to process and recognize natural language and create conversational experiences.

For decades, we have seen movies like "War Games" and "The Terminator" that led us to imagine a world where we can talk to machines...and they take over the world and destroy it. Now, machines have reached the point that they are beginning to learn how to process our natural language. Voice is great! But voice alone is not innovation, our ability to understand natural language is.

Is it perfect? No! Far from it. We are feverishly teaching machines to do something that has taken us thousands of years to perfect: communication and language. Every language, culture, and person has nuances in how they speak. Voice is so error-prone today because of the individual subjectivity of communication styles. Google tracked how many ways people performed the task of setting an alarm, which is just one simple action. Guess how many ways people set an alarm with our voices? 5,000. It is not easy to program subjectivity.

We will get there but it's important to remember that this is just the beginning of our journey with voice but the opportunity is awe-inspiring and massive!

The compounded annual voice growth rate is 121.3%[86]. The Voice Commerce (vCommerce) market is estimated to be between a $45[87] -$80[8] billion market by 2023.

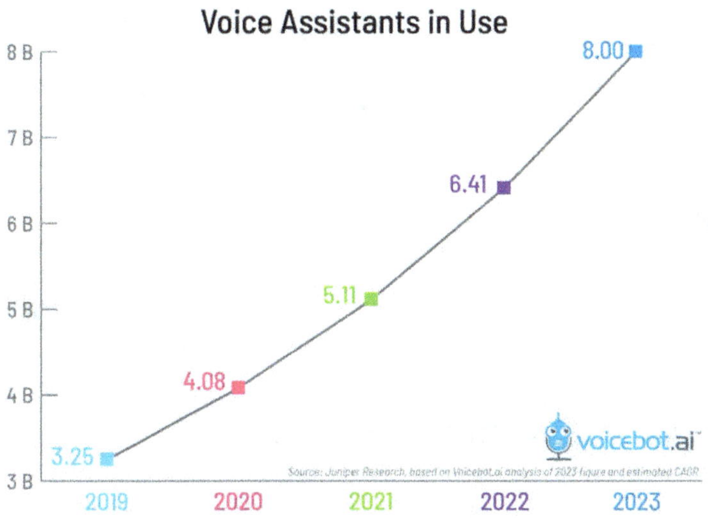

Source: Voicebot.ai, Voice Assistants in Use[88]

Say OK Google - Talk to Discovered Book – 3.25 Billion Voice Assistants

According to Juniper Research, there will be over 8 billion voice devices in use by 2023[8]. **8 BILLION!** I have cited as much of the free research I could in this book but you can purchase the full research report for $4044 USD, €3546, or £2990[89]. There is a less expensive report for a few hundred dollars less with less data.

[86] *Say OK Google - Talk to Discovered Book – Voice Growth*

[87] *Say OK Google - Talk to Discovered Book – $45 Billion Voice*

[89] *Say OK Google - Talk to Discovered Book – Juniper Paid Research*

Voice Adoption Rate Comparison

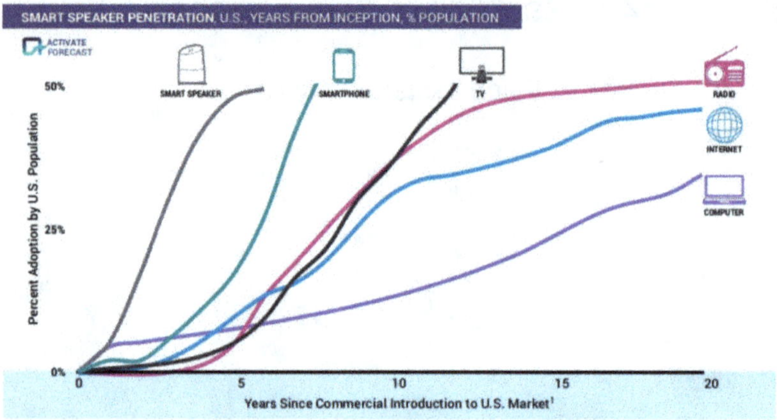

Source: Activate Tech & Media Outlook 2018[90]

Say OK Google - Talk to Discovered Book – Voice Adoption

The adoption rate of voice has superseded that of the Internet and smartphones **combined**. I personally believe that this is because voice is the first interface we don't have to learn to use. Every demographic has adopted voice quickly from people just learning language (aka toddlers) to people who have spoken languages for half a century (aka Baby Boomers). We don't have to learn to speak but every other interface involves a learning curve.

- Search - We had to dumb things down to find the answer. We almost had to unlearn some of the things that we knew about language until the search engines caught up to become discovery engines.
- Web - Pretty big learning curve, primarily around how to find information. Even today you still have to scan a site quickly to learn it. Too complex? I'm out. Consumers will spend three to five seconds looking for something, in general.

- Mobile - This probably entailed the biggest learning curve to the smartphone's interface. In fact, many Baby Boomers call their smartphones "dumb phones," which is hilarious. People often try to double tap (like a double click of a Windows mouse) or think of old behaviors from computers and tried to replicate that behavior on a smartphone. But we had to learn new behaviors like swipe, pinch to zoom, and new interactions we never had to perform before.

Consumer Awareness of Voice

During February 2018, PwC surveyed a nationally representative sample of 1,000 Americans between the ages of 18-64 who have access to the internet via an online survey conducted by a leading global research firm. A month later, they also conducted two focus group sessions.

Only 10% of surveyed respondents were not familiar with voice-enabled products and devices. Of the 90% who were, the majority had used a voice assistant (72%). Adoption is being driven by younger consumers, households with children, and households with an income of $100,000 or more[12].

When asked, "Have your spoken or issued voice commands...", the answers may be a bit surprising.

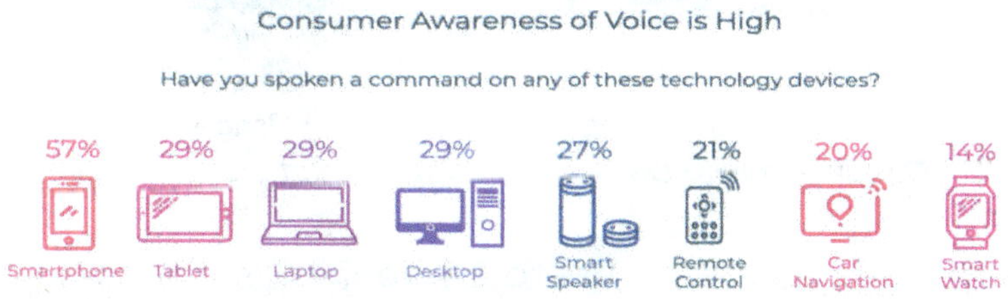

Source: PwC, Prepare for the Voice Revolution[91]

Say OK Google - Talk to Discovered Book - Voice Awareness

Most people assume voice is just limited to smart speakers and mobile phones but there are dozens of device platforms and that number is growing quickly as the Internet of Things (IOT) category grows to integrate smart and voice tech.

Voice Speaker & Mobile Usage

Despite being accessible everywhere, three out of every four consumers (74%) are using their mobile voice assistants at home. The majority of focus group participants were quick to say that they prefer privacy when speaking to their voice assistant and that using it in public "just looks weird."

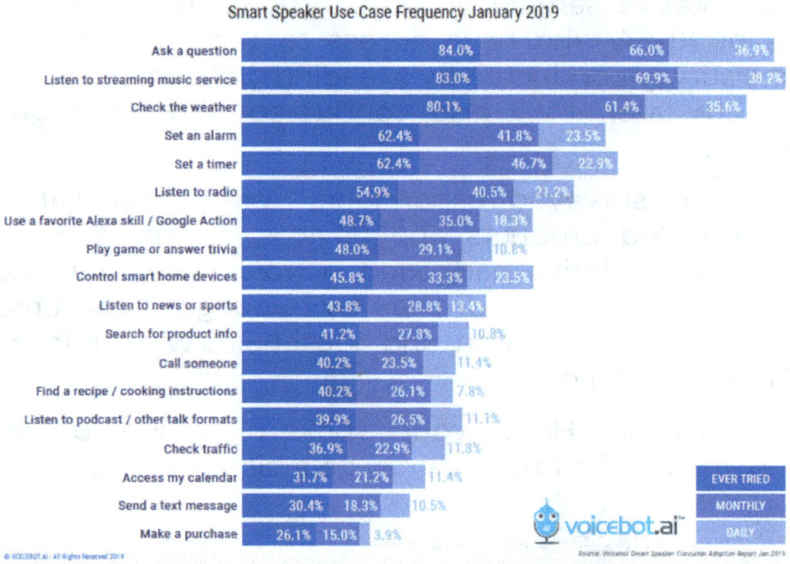

Source: Voicebot.ai, Smart Speaker Usage[92]

Say OK Google - Talk to Discovered Book – Smart Speaker Voice Usage

This could explain why 18- to 24-year-olds are using their voice assistants less, since this age group tends to spend more time outside the home.

Smart Speaker vs Mobile Usage of Voice Assistants

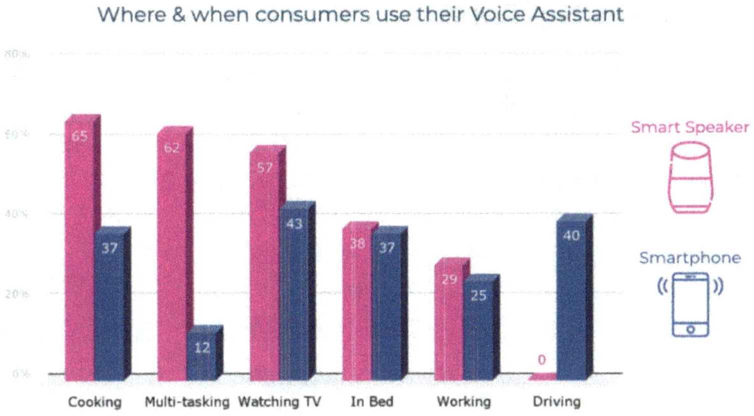

Source: PwC - Prepare for the Voice Revolution[93]

Say OK Google - Talk to Discovered Book - Smartphone Voice Usage

With the consistent rapid growth on voice, this leaves brands very little time to plan and respond later.

> Brands cannot afford to take a wait and see posture with voice.

It is more important for your brand to start now and set the expectation that the first phase will be to begin and learn. Right now, the brand that is first to the dance is most likely to get discovered by the shopper. There may or may not be a way to displace the incumbent voice winner with ads, a better voice experience, or something else, but we won't know until that happens.

New Behaviors Not Replaced Behaviors

One mistake people often make is thinking that voice is replacing an old behavior. Voice is adding *new behaviors* that we need to pay attention to, it is not replacing a behavior that we no longer need to worry about.

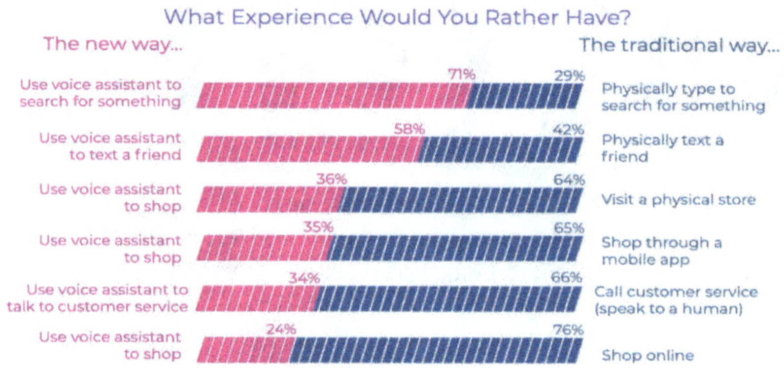

Source: PwC, Prepare for the Voice Revolution[94]
Say OK Google - Talk to Discovered Book – Prefer Voice

Voice Search

Voice search is one of the most popular use cases yet it is often misunderstood. Voice search does not replace traditional search. In fact, search on desktop and mobile continues to climb. Voice search is a new behavior -- one that is rapidly becoming an extremely popular search and discovery behavior. This is a HUGE opportunity for brands to capture new shopper attention when they are in the research and discovery phase and a way to build brand affinity with a delightful voice experience for existing customers.

Second Screening

Voice helps you take advantage of second screening, which is when you are watching something on TV and searching for an answer (often related to what's on the TV) on your mobile device. We have seen that people often use their voice assistant, as opposed to typing in a traditional search window when second screening. This is a potentially fantastic voice opportunity for popular series and shows. Watching "The Bachelorette" and you want to cyber stalk your favorite Bachelor, you may ask a few questions about him. Who is John from "The Bachelorette?" Where does John work? Has John ever been married? Many brands have created interesting ways to piggyback off of trending shows, movies, and character licensing trends.

Voice Assistants

Voice experiences can be created for research and discovery, vCommerce[16], or customer service-related experiences.

We are starting to have access to more data that is helping us navigate consumer behavior. According to the PwC's Consumer Intelligence Series voice assistants survey, voice assistants are beginning to have more influence over purchases.

44% of consumers have used their voice assistant **to control other household devices.**

Consumers That Used a Voice Assistant to Control Another Device

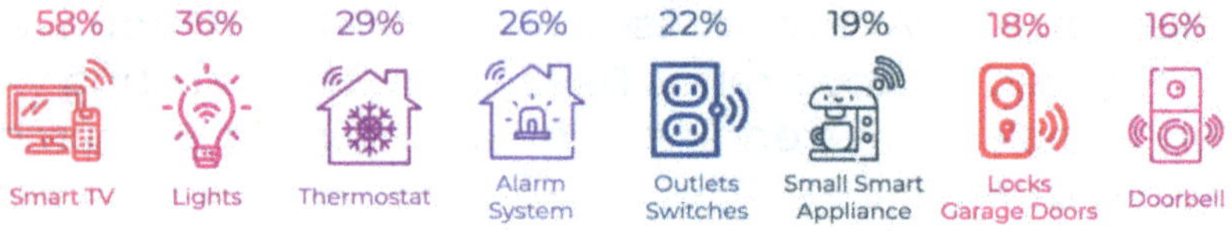

Source: PwC, Prepare for the Voice Revolution[95]

Say OK Google - Talk to Discovered Book – Voice Assistant Control

Kmart, which still operates 200 stores in Australia and New Zealand, created a gift-giving voice skill that helps shoppers find a gift. The voice experience guides customers through an in-depth shopping experience[96]:

- Tell the voice assistant the person you are shopping for (my husband or a 9-year-old boy, for example);
- Tell the voice assistant your budget;
- Based on the information you provide, the selection will then off you a couple of suggestions.

But here is where is gets really cool. Based on your home location (on your Alexa) or your GPS, if you are using your smartphone, the voice assistant will check if the

---

[96] *Say OK Google - Talk to Discovered Book – KMart*

suggested gift is in stock and available at the closest store. If not, it will tell you the closest store!

They launched the skill in October and got pretty good traction during the holiday shopping season but the traffic spiked in January. The First Agency, who built the skill, saw an increase in all of their voice skills in January. They attributed the increase due to the highest smart speaker sales quarter in history.

The retention and return rate of the shoppers to the skill ranged between 30-60%, which I think is fantastic for a well-designed experience.

Another important consideration is attribution of voice to sales. Today you can buy through voice but there are still a few bugs to iron out to make it fully frictionless. This will also improve with time but it is another risk of forcing voice projects to have an ROI.

What the team didn't expect to see was customer service queries. They heard questions about return policies, store inquiries, and other customer service questions. When you create a powerful voice experience, shoppers trust the brand. The experience data can help your brand deliver even better experiences based on what people value and ask of your brand.

Oh Lord!

You can use voice to create new behaviors and experiences to interact with your brand. The Church of England in London launched a voice skill on Alexa and got more than 75,000 questions in the first year[97]. They connected this to GPS and search and the skill was able to recommend a church near them. Here are some of their learnings:

---

[97] *Say OK Google - Talk to Discovered Book – Oh Lord!*

- 40% asked for a prayer;
- 31% followed the device's voice experience to explore Christian faith more;
- 16% asked for a reflection on Easter;
- 7% asked for a church near them;
- 6% asked for a daily prayer before their meal.

The most powerful point is that 4,500 new people integrated this voice experience into their ***daily lives.***

It's important to understand that the experience you may have to build may be one that people don't yet do, understand, or think they need – but once you do, they won't want to live without it.

Better Voice Experiences

Before we start to talk about how awesome voice is, let's talk about some of the challenges that we have to face when it comes to using voice speakers and all of the super cool voice-assisted technologies.

It's easy for us to forget how awful the Internet was when it first came out. Do you remember getting AOL discs in the mail every single day and you'd have to install America Online to connect your phone line to your computer. You had the pleasure of listening to the modem sounds screeching as dial-up connection was established to the Internet. It was painful and slow.

Once you finally got connected to the Internet, then you had to wait several minutes, not seconds, for the Internet to load. Some pages would load so unbelievably slowly -- starting at the top of the page and just loading images pixel by pixel until the entire page was loaded. You literally created habits to numb the impatience, like making yourself a pot of coffee, fixing your cup, and skimming the daily newspapers. Yes, newspapers were still around when the internet was penetrating U.S. households.

Because we become so accustomed to the speed of technology, our attention span has decreased from a 30-second commercial spot to about three seconds.

When Siri first came out, you would see all these sensational commercials about this amazing voice assistant that could help you out with anything your heart desired. And you may have been one of the people who tried to use her, and it didn't work out so well... Most times, she didn't recognize what you said or even worse, she did something that was completely opposite of what you requested.

Today, Siri most likely can answer any question. But sometimes the experience isn't the best because she often shows you the top search results on Google. This often results in you tapping your phone, which kind of defeats the whole purpose of a delightful, *hands-free*, voice experience, doesn't it?

What you have to understand is inherently machines aren't smart alone, we have to teach the voice assistant machine how to deliver a smart conversation. We have human subjectivity that is not easily translated and programmed to a machine. Subjectivity has too many variables. There's no subjectivity when it comes to how voice machines work and how they process.

We are expecting a robot to understand all the nuances of natural language and you can't easily program nuances.

A perfect example is if you are making a reservation for dinner, and the person asks you how many people are in your party? Then a natural response for me would be myself and my husband. My husband and I aren't a number.

Human:

Bethanie and her dashingly handsome hubby = Party of 2 people

Robot:

1+1=2

Bethanie and her dashingly handsome husband aren't a number, they are the names of people, I think = Party of 0 people

The (machine) voice assistant is listening for a numbered response. I gave her my answer, which is two people (my husband and I). We are human beings and I know we are two people. But how would a machine know that? It wouldn't.

We can program for a majority of the nuances that we think people have. We just have to be thoughtful of how people may engage and interact with us on voice. A perfect example is answering a yes/ no question.

Here are possible ways we may answer "yes:"

- Yes
- Yeah
- Yea
- Yep
- Uh huh
- For sure
- Definitely
- Yaaaaas
- Affirmative
- Nodding the head up and down (it happens)

We do our best to program for what we expect. However, sometimes how we interact and respond is not predictable. Set the expectation that your voice journey begins with experimentation. Voice is an iterative learning process that we can improve but will never master because people and our behaviors will always evolve. We have to have a mindset to always be optimizing and adapting.

Over the last several years, the dominant players on the voice landscape have included Amazon with Alexa and Google with Google Assistant and now Google Home. Both companies are scrambling to understand natural language as quickly as possible.

Although Apple was first to the game, Amazon led the market, and Google has made the most progress adapting and understanding language. At this point Google has a 95% success rate with English speaking languages. Amazon is second and Apple continues to lag behind them both. Even though Apple is the last in the race right now, they have made several key acquisitions of voice companies. We predict that Apple will soon open up Siri voice development tools to its massive app developer network to bring the life back into Siri.

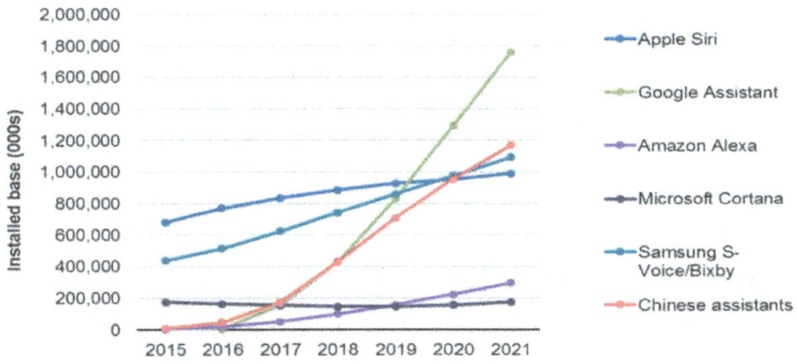

Source: Ovum, Virtual digital assistants take over the world by 2021[98]
Say OK Google - Talk to Discovered Book – Voice Takes Over

With the rapid advancements, voice is now mass and it's time that every brand took a serious look at the potential the voice could bring for your business.

Voice Assistants

Most of us are familiar with Alexa. Alexa has skills, which are like mini-apps that deliver an experience on Alexa. As of January 2019, there are 80,000+ skills.

With Google, there is something similar to Alexa skills called Actions, which allow people to interact with a brand or a business simply through a voice command. Actions by Google are invoked on voice search and Google Assistant on smart speakers and smart phones.

With Actions by Google, here are some cool things you can do:

- Perform a Google Search
- Ask for directions on Google Maps
- Create routines (morning routines, smart home routines)
- Order coffee (Starbucks)
- Order flowers (1-800-Flowers)
- Learn how to save money (Citi)
- Sell goods and services
- Tell your phone to perform an action
- Call someone
- Open apps on your phone
- Unlock your Pixel phone
- Play music (Google Play, Spotify, Pandora)
- Listen to a podcast
- Check the weather
- Open a website page
- You can even find Santa!

Facebook also has a voice interface on Facebook portal devices. At CES 2019 (an annual gathering that focuses on consumer technology, Facebook's Chief AI Scientist Yann

LeCun casually mentioned that, "Facebook would be interested in is offering smart digital assistants — something that has a level of common sense[99]."

After Facebook made the move to shut down M, the mobile messenger assistant, Mark Zuckerberg confirmed what may journalists predicted, with Facebook's position on voice[100], "You can look at where the product roadmap is likely to go on this and see why this would be a very useful and an important way where people are going to want to interact with more technology that way." If you want to hear more about this, simply skip to 46:48 to listen to the question and answer about voice[99].

Voice is quickly becoming a part of our daily lives from smart speakers in our homes, to voice assistants in our cars, watches, and smartphones when we are on the go. As voice moves to the forefront of our marketing plans, brands are building new voice skills, actions, and assistants to connect deeper with consumers across the voice platforms.

---

[99] *Say OK Google - Talk to Discovered Book – Facebook AI*

[100] *Say OK Google - Talk to Discovered Book – Facebook Shareholders*

VOICE SEARCH

Voice search offers a potentially huge opportunity for marketers right now. Rebecca Sentance of eConsultancy, estimates are that voice search was closer to 13% of Google's total search volume and 20% of mobile search volume in 2018 as Google has previously stated. SEO Tribunal says total Google searches in 2018 were 2 trillion, so combining these figures suggests over **250 billion voice searches were conducted last year**. All data so far indicates this number will continue to rise at staggering rates[5].

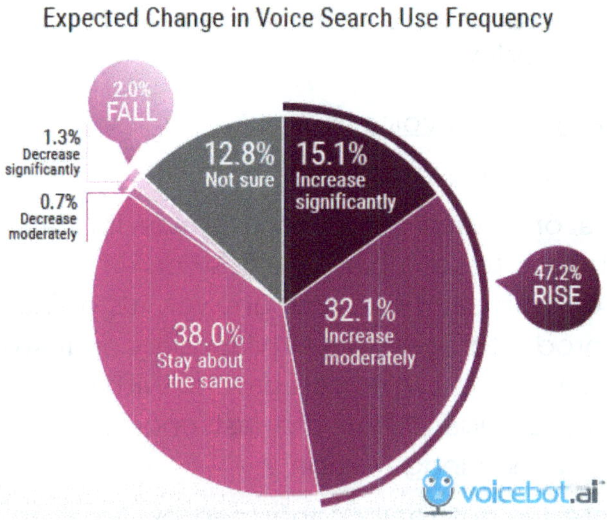

Source: Voicebot.ai, Voice Assistant SEO Report for Brands[110]

Say OK Google - Talk to Discovered Book – Voice Search Prediction

Regardless of what stat you read, the same may not apply to your brand or your shoppers. You will have to create your own baseline metrics with voice to measure for your business and your shoppers. We have seen between 10-40% search happen on voice compared to similar searches made with more traditional methods.

With the voice market expanding so rapidly and the barrier to entry on the voice channel is incredibly low. But just because it's easy to enter the voice market right now doesn't mean that every brand should rush to get a crappy voice experience to market so they can win. That risks the value of voice as a channel and can negatively affect growth, trust, and, ultimately, commerce.

I'm not sure how much you personally use your voice assistant or voice search on your smartphone, but you may have asked a question recently that could not be answered. Does that mean that there's no answer anywhere on the whole world wide web to that question? Not really. Let's explore what we believe is happening on voice search today.

How Alexa Searches Voice

If you are asking Alexa a question:

1. Amazon is first going to examine its native answer database to search for the answer.
2. If Amazon can't find that answer, it's going to look in its product pages for a similar query or answer.
3. If it can't find it in its database or within the millions of product pages, then the last choice is to Microsoft Bing's Knowledge Graph.

This last step is not really confirmed by Amazon officially, just based on what we've seen and tested personally. More times than not, Amazon will go to Bing's Knowledge Graph for an answer.

How Siri Searches Voice

1. Listens to what you ask and sends the request to Apple's servers for translation.
2. Takes that request and attempts to fulfil it.
3. In the case of a search for a business, the search agent will usually automatically localize that request – so you might say "Find me a plumber," but Siri will assume "Find me a plumber" + local to me.
4. To fulfil your search, Siri will usually ask Google. Google will then look at its own databases, search results, local results, local business and any local business reviews it may have access to in order to provide these results (aka Schema).
5. Siri also looks at other resources, like Yelp.
6. Having done all this work in more or less real time, the search agent then has a little think, synthesizes the data, and delivers you an answer.

How Google Assistant Searches Voice

If you are asking the Google Assistant a question:

Google has the biggest search advantage of the other two because she pretty much owns search. Google has more answers than Apple and Amazon.

1. Google looks at it's platform channels first (Google My Business, Local Product Inventory, Express Shopping, Voice Actions or Apps)
2. Checks Search – Ideally looking for a response that is in Position 0 or is the Featured Snippet (aka the Answer Box)
3. Checks Schema

Google considers voice search an "eyes free technology" meaning you should be able to get the answer by hearing and you should have to look, tap, or click. Google released their The Evaluation of Search Speech Guidelines[111]. Google Assistant needs its own guidelines in place, as many of its interactions utilize what is called "eyes-free technology," when there is no screen as part of the experience. This is the case with many smart speakers, there is no screen. Your answer has to be satisfying by speech. When there is a screen the number of answers seem to vary. These variables will be design considerations when creating your voice customer experiences.

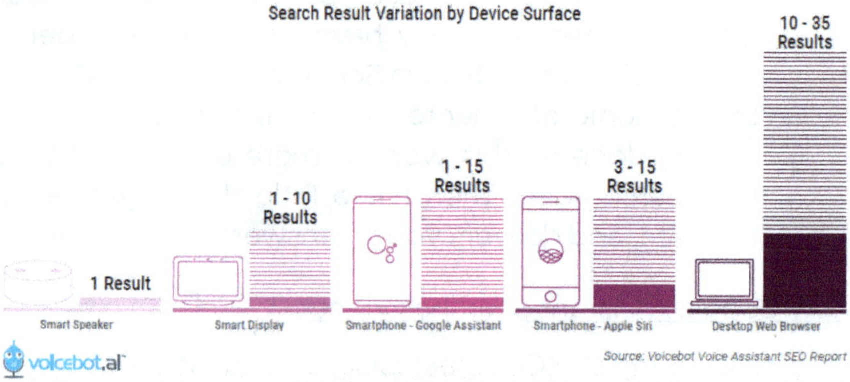

Source: Voicebot.ai, Voice Assistant SEO Report for Brands[112]
Say OK Google - Talk to Discovered Book – Voice Results Vary

What does that mean if you ask a question and none of these platforms can answer the question?

That means it's an opportunity.

Most likely, Schema doesn't exist for that question. Google has millions and millions of opportunities for your brand to win on Schema, which could also translate into winning on voice.

---

[111] *Say OK Google - Talk to Discovered Book – Evaluation of Speech*

To illustrate this, let me give you a baby example. As a mom of a new baby, I can't tell you how many questions I asked because I didn't know the answer. Let's just talk about food.

I would ask TONS of questions:

- What type of baby food should I feed my baby?
- How do I make my own organic baby food? (definitely a first baby question)
- What type of chemicals are in baby food?
- What should a baby at 6 months (7, 8, 9,10...) eat?
- Plus thousands more.

That was just for the baby stage of life. When they started to eat solid foods, I would ask questions about what food a toddler should have and so on.

I learned later through a client who sells baby food that there are certain solid foods that your baby shouldn't transition to and one of them was little orange fish, which I gave my kids plenty of when they started eating solid foods. Apparently, that solid snack is not good because it's pretty much just fillers and sodium. Another #1 Mom moment right there.

As a parent who was obsessed with healthier food options for my infant, because the brand had superior placement of their product on an end cap or with a shelf talker, I bought it. I just knew it was a small snack-sized food, I just assumed it was safe and I bought it as one of their snacks.

If your brand serves overwhelmed, busy shoppers with education so they can make the right decision, then imagine how many voice questions and opportunities your brand has to educate while influencing the path to purchase? A ton!

If you take my state of mind as a new mom and know that what's most important to me is making healthy choices for my new baby's body, our conversation can be incredibly impactful to my sanity and my peace of mind. I am now emotionally vested in a brand that helped me be a better mom! Talk about ways to nurture brand affinity, loyalty, and advocacy.

I always felt like I needed help and who did I trust? Search. Before you judge me, yes, I would call my mom or my mother-in-law but that was only if I had the time to talk. If I needed a quick answer, Google would be my go-to every time. And I'm not alone: 84% of people trust online reviews more than those of their friends and family[113].

Voice as an advocate

When considering voice, how can your brand become your consumer's teacher, advocate, confidant, and loyal friend? Your voice conversation becomes an unbreakable bond between the brand and the consumer. Brands can connect with your consumer's state of mind, their intent, AND their desires. You have created the opportunity to reach and nurture shoppers across every phase of the buying journey and well after they've bought. You can turn complete strangers into disciples who will excitedly advocate for your brand without ever being asked to do so.

Imagine your brand's position with me as a new mom and who do you think I will go to later? The brand that helped and guided me when I was in need. Who do you think I will turn to first when my toddler gets of age for solid foods? The brand that empowered me when I felt confused and helpless.

With great power comes great responsibility. Since your brand now knows the stage and age of my children, it is your duty and your responsibility to continue to add value to our lives if you want me to continue to buy your products.

---

[113] *Say OK Google - Talk to Discovered Book – Trusting Strangers*

Voice should always help:

- Save shoppers time
- Save shoppers money
- Make shoppers lives easier
- Reduce the friction in the customer experience, not just the buying journey
- Educate, delight, and surprise
- Accomplish my goal hands-free

Voice allows your brand to be discovered through consumer intent and continue the relationship from stage to stage in a conversational and meaningful way.

Yes, right now, I'm saying opportunity is virtually limitless because it really is. You have an opportunity to create such a strong bond with your consumers that, no matter how much money your competition has to displace you, it doesn't matter because you cannot be displaced or replaced.

If you are an emerging brand, voice is a way to beat your biggest competitor **without out-ad-spending them.**

Every time you hear, "I'm sorry, I don't know how to answer that yet, I'm still learning," I get super excited. Like happy dance excited. it is an opportunity to fulfill an intent with your brand's unique brand voice in a way that no one else is doing right now.

I think it's worth repeating that less than 1% of brands are doing Schema properly. Voice answer and discovery engines all appear to use and trust Google or Schema. For the hundreds of categories, **the opportunity is wide open**. The barrier to entry is so incredibly low, it's almost laughable.

But this opportunity is not going to be open like this forever. In fact, in a comparison of voice questions and answers from July 2018 to January 2019, Google reduced unanswered questions by 21%. They are scrambling to get the best answers to deliver the best voice experience.[114]

All the sections you see in bright red below returned **no response**, meaning it couldn't be answered.

[114] *Say OK Google - Talk to Discovered Book – Voice Answers Report*

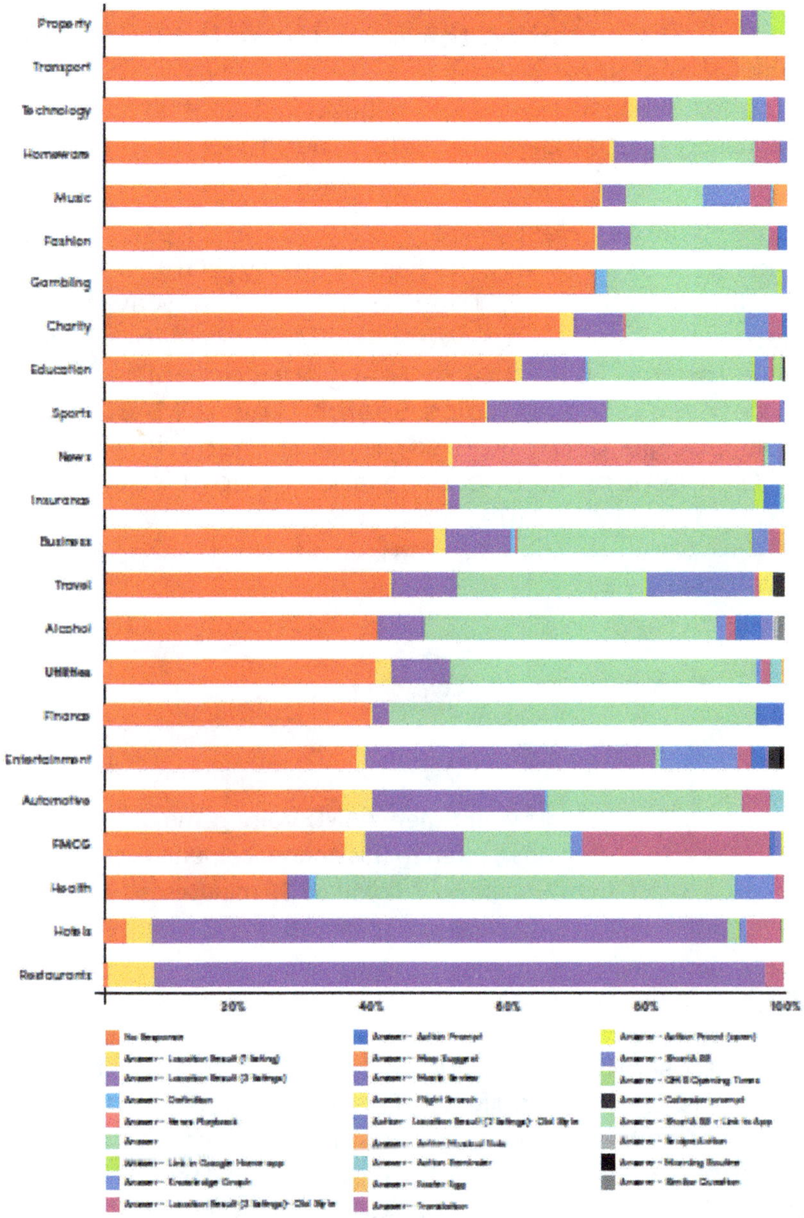

Source: Rabbit and Pork, Voice Search Ranking Report[115]

Say OK Google - Talk to Discovered Book – Voice Answers Image

Brands are also starting to realize the revenue lost due to a lack of visibility on voice search. A "New York Times" bestseller publishing house realized that it stood to lose $17 million in just a few months because their books are not being found through voice search[10].

Google wants desperately to fulfill these question requests with answers. In fact, in May 2019, at Google's Next I/O conference, they announced a way to apply Schema easily to your website FAQ and your How To Videos (on YouTube too) so that your content is found on Google Assistant and Voice Search. This is MAJOR. Super Major. Google had taken something that will answer 10, 20, 30 questions at one time and made it easy for you. Google gets more questions answered on voice search and you win because you knew about this opportunity. You're welcome.

To start your Schema AND Voice game right now, listen to this announcement from Google now. **It will be 36 minutes well spent. I promise.**[116]

Even with so many questions still unanswered, the value outweighs the frustrations. The good news is that most consumers expect some bumps in the road and are pretty forgiving and willing to try a couple more times for an answer. I expect this will change as Google and brands get more advanced and build better voice experiences. This is another reason why a well thought out voice experience is critical to the success of your voice strategy long term.

The typical voice user will make 3 attempts to get answers on voice before abandoning.

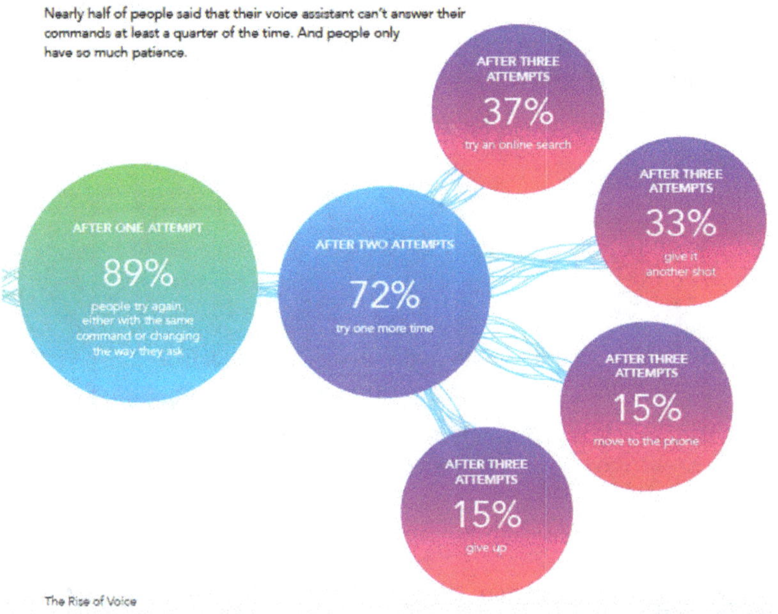

Source: Invoca, The Rise of Voice Report[117]

Say OK Google - Talk to Discovered Book – No Answer Attempts

Search is changing and moving from a keyword to an intent, we must now understand how language plays a part. SEO is still important but now with new considerations of optimizing for needs, intent, and voice.

Most of us are used to thinking about search in terms of keywords. Keywords to me would be the best shampoo for curly hair, the best sushi restaurant in Atlanta, or simple steps to changing a car battery. Keywords are just simple everyday quick queries. You would never have a conversation with a person and say "shampoo for curly hair?" Or "best sushi restaurant?" When you think about voice, think about the natural conversation that people have.

You'll hear terms like NLU, which is natural language understanding, which means translating human language into structured data so machines can understand it. You may also hear semantic or speakable, which is the context or how we put things in speakable terms. Speaking in "speakable terms" may seem like it's an easy thing but it can be rather difficult to wrap your head around.

Create voice experiences that feel like a conversation with a person. **A fun, engaging, and memorable share-worthy human conversation.**

Start by thinking about your content and the searchability of your content in terms of speakable, how you would naturally ask or answer a question. If you ever asked a voice assistant or speaker a question in a very natural human way but the response that you're given was read like it was out of a super advanced textbook, then it probably didn't answer your question at all. It could have made you more confused and ruined the experience for you as a consumer. You may have asked the questions in a more search engine-ish manner to get a better (and more human) response.

Ultimately, the way that you've done things for years has to change to prepare your content and your sites and your pages for speakable, natural language and conversations. We have to evolve again. Isn't it fun?

There are some rules that we can attribute back to school that will help us during this process of navigating into the voice world.

Here's a quick example:

Voice Question: *Do pigs eat watermelon rinds?*

Voice Answer: *No.*

If you have a website page that answers that specific question with the answer no, how useful is that? Not so much.

Here is a better answer:

No pigs do not eat watermelon rinds because they can't digest the hard shell of the watermelon. Instead, you could feed the pigs lettuce, slop, garbage, and (whatever else pigs eat...).

That is a more valuable response to a question! This is a fantastic question if your brand happens to sell pig slop in pig digestible containers! This question could be one of many questions in the customer journey. Then, the next natural step could be researching alternatives to feed pigs, other than watermelon rinds. After you answer the watermelon question, you should move them forward to the next touchpoint in their journey.

From there you could prompt the consumer to see if they are a new pig owner or had just adopted a new pig family member.

Here's what you could say to find out if they do have a new little piggie at home.

Continuation of the voice conversation:

"Many of our customers don't know what to feed their new piglet family member and we created this New Little Piggie Guide for new pig owners when they're trying to find the right food for their new family piglet. Would you

like me to send you the guide or would you prefer to watch it in a video??"

That is just one example of how we have a conversation as people. There is nothing robotic about it. There's nothing that feels unnatural; it feels like a conversation because it is.

Don't worry if you're thinking about all of the stuff that you have to rewrite or you have to look at and determine if it's ready for speakable terms. We are just scratching the surface of considerations, not necessarily things that are urgent for you to do right now.

PRO TIP:

If you have a FAQ page, that may be a great place to start for voice search optimization. **Check to see if your questions and responses are phrased the way you would ask a friend of family member. If you wrote them, ask someone else to review them for you.**

People turn to voice search (and online search) for everything you can imagine. We all go to search to ask questions and get answers. We are getting more and more specific, which could mean several variations of questions if your widget solves many problems. Or if you are super laser niche focused, people may be looking for your super niche answer.

FAQs are a super powerful way to get started while building credibility and authority with clear, concise answers.

Here are the categories and the frequency on smart speakers:

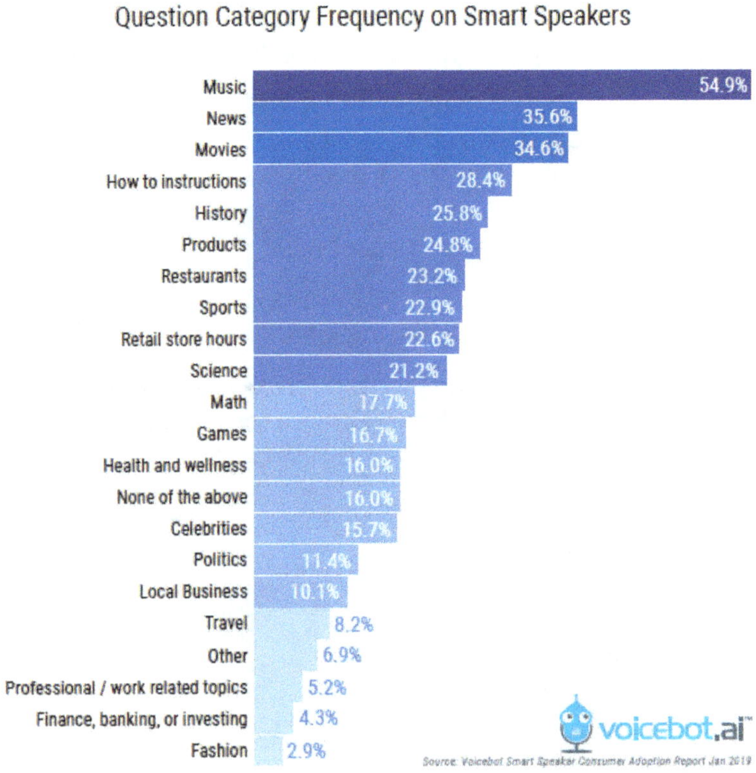

Source: Voicebot.ai, Smart Speaker Consumer Adoption Report (01/19)[118]
Say OK Google - Talk to Discovered Book – Consumer Voice Questions

One thing that is important to understand is there is only one winner in this voice search game (on smart speakers, which is still 30+ million device market today). If you think of page 1 of Google as a team, let's say that position 0 (answer box or featured snippets) is the #1 draft pick. You want that #1 draft pick spot first. Secondarily, position 1, 2, and 3 on the search results page 1 on Google. Sure, there may be other players that deserve to be on the team but nobody talks about them and positions 4 and below don't get the visibility, big contracts, or endorsement deals.

Everyone else that's on the team, gets to participate but doesn't get the same rewards of the top players. That is how search rewards star players, too. The best player may be on the bench. Just as the best solution may be on page 8 of Google search results. Because they are benched on page 8, no one will ever see them play.

On page 1 of Google search results, 75% of the traffic goes to the top three players. **75%!** Everybody else on the page just gets a participation trophy, not organic traffic or visibility in front on their shoppers.

Whoever provides the best answer will win. There are no other players who get to participate.

Right now, you cannot advertise on voice. You can't out-ad the answer. If you have an opportunity to be the answer on voice, why would you not do that right now?

VOICE CUSTOMER EXPERIENCES

One of the most powerful things about voice is our ability to mine conversational data. From day one, we begin to learn from your voice conversations with your shoppers. You will have greater insight and intelligence into the conversations that shoppers ***want to have with your brand.*** You can then expand your voice experience to cover the conversational interactions with your shoppers that they yearn to have. You may have visibility to the touchpoints that you could only guess about in the past. This is an incredibly powerful aspect of voice. Your brand has the ability to hear what consumers are actually saying during their interactions on voice.

Could you validate what consumers say or do on the customer journey today? Sure, but a majority of it is manual or entails multiple disparate solutions. You could run surveys, focus groups, and actual interviews with customers. There are some automated systems to help you record and capture what is happening online like Hotjar, Heap, FullStory, MixPanel, Google Analytics, and more. There is a reason there are more than 7,000 Martech software applications in existence. The marketing struggle is real.

Voice gives you the ability to capture and gather data intelligently by having voice conversations with your consumers directly.

We all make assumptions based on:

- Our bias, both consciously and, even worse, unconsciously.
- Our past experiences.
- Best of all, our gut and instinct.

Sometimes we're close to correct and other times we are way off base. We're doing the best we can based on the data that we have. Being able to make better decisions for our brand or organization is what most of us want to do.

Voice changes that game. Here are a few examples of what voice allows you to do:

- Start a conversation with your consumers with your best assumption possible of the conversation that you think consumers want to have with your brand.
- Create an engaging emotional connection between your consumers and your brand.
- See and hear the pieces of the conversation that you're missing. Your brand could be missing:
- Customer experience opportunities
    - Sales opportunities
    - Engagement opportunities
    - Brand awareness
    - Brand affinity and loyalty opportunities
    - Advocacy opportunities

For the first time ever, you can create an engaging and dynamic conversation with your consumer within the voice channel. Even better, this gives you the chance to validate your assumptions with your consumers directly. The voice machines and assistants are learning how to create a deeper bond that is more meaningful with your consumers as you collect data. Data in the form of questions, responses, emotions, and sentiment from the voice of your consumers.

The anti-glass slipper

Here's a quick scenario of how this can play out.

A particular brand, Antonia Saint NY was launching a technology that would allow you to capture video images of your feet[125]. That technology would then create a custom shoe made just for your foot. In this project, they were going to market with a Kickstarter crowdfunding campaign. This is a great (but time-consuming) way to validate any concept or idea. They planned to crowdsource and raise money based on the market response to this idea.

Initially, the team assumed that the demographic that wanted this custom shoe was women – busy working women who lived in cities with public transit or who walked quite a bit, women who wanted to look stylish and fashionable but wanted comfort as they stood on their feet all day long. They needed to look good for their 9 a.m. meeting and equally as good for their 6 p.m. happy hour.

Ladies, what shoes offer function and fashion? Exactly. For my comfy Dr. Scholl's lovin' men, the answer is: none. Fellas, just imagine something really painful clenching your feet all day long as you walk from meeting to meeting and to lunch and on and on. You still have to show up somewhere at the end of the day, after you're tired from walking all day. At this point, your feet are pretty much just numb from the pain. You don't know what you dread more, walking to the high-top table to meet your party or daring to slip your shoes off when you sit down. There is a very likely chance your dogs swell up and you can't get your shoes back on and have to walk barefoot, carrying those fashionable shoes. Been there, done that. No shame. My women friends understand completely.

---

[125] *Say OK Google - Talk to Discovered Book – Anti-glass slipper*

Back to business case. They decided to rapidly test demographics to Facebook, prior to launching the U.S. campaign. They created a series of ads testing their ideas with different creative and different copy. They targeted many women of different ages, in different metropolitan cities to understand if this was the problem women would be willing to pay to solve.

They rapidly tested 70 demographics within a few weeks. It was going OK but not as well as they hoped. The team came up with an idea to test a new community and demographic: men. They removed the filter that excluded men from the targeting, then something magical happened: Conversions and engagement went through the roof. It was like a Facebook marketer's dream.

They learned the winning demographic was nothing like the women persona they had created. It was actually transgender men. They modified the Facebook ad with creative and copy to appeal to transgender men, who were struggling to find comfortable, fashionable shoes to fit their larger feet.

The project fundraising goal was to raise a couple hundred thousand dollars to fund the first round of shoe development and production. Originally, the shoes were priced at $250 per pair.

While my experience in marketing would have also led me to focus on women, the community of the transgender men was completely underserved and in need of this solution. And most importantly, they would pay (handsomely) to solve it. They found the perfect demographic based on the problem. With the support of several thousand supporters, that Kickstarter project raised more than $1.8 million, much of it funded by transgender men eager for better footwear options[125].

As we make the best assumptions possible about the customer journey, about our demographic, and about the experience that consumers want to have our brands, we need to recognize that these can affect our bottom-line or potentially prevent an idea from ever becoming a reality in the first place.

When we talk about voice many people limit the use cases to smart speakers and smartphones but don't forget about the car, wearables and the other device platforms that voice assistance can be used.

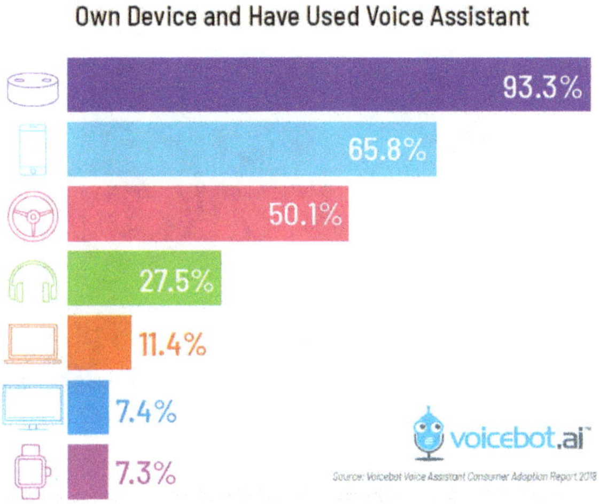

Source: Voicebot.ai, Smart Speaker Consumer Adoption Report[126]

Say OK Google - Talk to Discovered Book – Voice Device Usage

Voice can help you **understand which touchpoints exist that you hadn't ever considered.**

With new behaviors, come new touchpoints. Imagine the potential opportunities to engage with your shoppers in a meaningful way when we are in the middle of all of these different activities. Here are some of the activities people are doing when they activate and engage with their voice assistants.

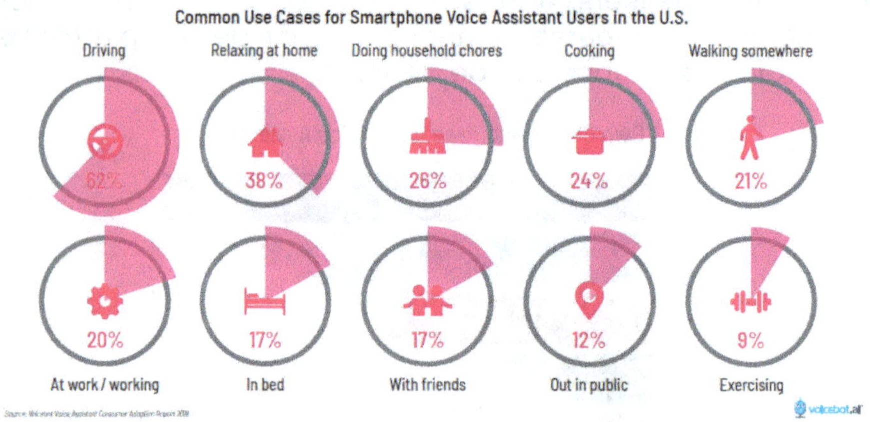

Source: Voicebot.ai, Voice Assistant Consumer Adoption Report[127]
Say OK Google - Talk to Discovered Book – Voice Activities

We have an amazing client, Paul Gaugin Cruises, that sells incredible luxury cruises. They are once-in-a-lifetime cruises through the South Pacific Islands[128]. They understand the experience that delights their customers once they've boarded the ship. Traveling with them is an unforgettable experience. Anyone that has ever cruised with them enjoys an exceptional experience.

The challenge is: What do your cruisers need to see, hear, and feel when consumers are solution-unaware? Imagine how many consumers don't even realize that the once-in-a-lifetime trip is actually a cruise through Tahiti and Fiji?

When people begin their voice journey, it always starts with a question. When planning a trip, people always have a lot of questions. The questions you ask when you plan a vacation may be very different from the questions I ask.

---

[128] *Say OK Google - Talk to Discovered Book – PG Cruises*

We both have the intent to plan an incredible vacation for our loved ones. We may both realize the solution is to take this luxurious cruise to the South Pacific on Paul Gauguin Cruises.

According to Think with Google, there are hundreds of touchpoints for everything from skin care to vacation planning. The brand that can thoughtfully answer the most questions for us during our decision-making process is most likely to win. It's not just about the intent, the answers, and the channel. It is also about reducing the friction and overcoming the consumer's objections easily and naturally though a conversation.

Travel planning may take more time to research than a typical purchase. It can take weeks and weeks to plan a big vacation. People are getting lazier and more accustomed to voice, so voice adoption rates are so high because it is easier to talk than type. If we can make any stage of the research, discovery, planning, and decision-making process easier for our consumers through a conversation that doesn't feel robotic, then we are light years ahead of most brands.

Once people become accustomed to using their voice, they use it more and more on a daily basis and the numbers continue to climb. 70% of smartphone owners have used their voice assistant in 2018. Up from 56% in 2017[129].

Smart Speaker vs Smartphone

Since we are now understanding a bit more about behavior, it is valuable to know where your shoppers may be activating your voice assistant. There have been varied opinions of the demographics to each speaker. I have

[129] *Say OK Google - Talk to Discovered Book – Voice Assistant Usage on Smartphones*

heard mid-high income buy Alexa or Walmart shoppers prefer Google. You can start with one platform and test it to see. Your approach and strategy may vary by brand, category, or use case depending on the objectives.

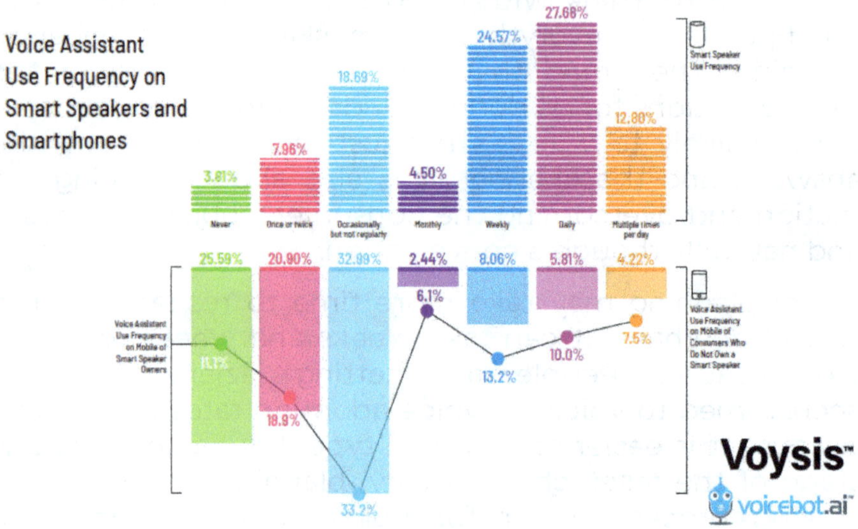

Source: Voicebot.ai, Voice Shopping Consumer Adoption Report[130]

Say OK Google - Talk to Discovered Book – Smart Speakers Battle Smartphones...FIGHT!

Every time I use voice as a consumer, my voice assistant learns more and more about how to engage with me in a meaningful way. That means learning about my preferences, my buying habits, and my shopping behaviors. I predict that as voice, machines, and neural learning mature, our voice experience will be less "War Games" and more "Minority Report."

My voice assistant will always be learning:

- That I feed my family healthy options and organic options;
- Which answer (and content) I engage with;
- What things I need to see or hear or do before I add

to cart or check out;

- What I buy and how often I buy it;
- How I pay for what I buy;
- How I manage my shopping lists and wish lists;
- Where I visit and how often I go there;
- I'm planning a trip and I'm looking at Fiji and South Africa.

There are limitless opportunities to create new customer experiences and behaviors with your shoppers. Here is a list of the most common smart speaker behavior and how frequency people seem to exhibit those behaviors:

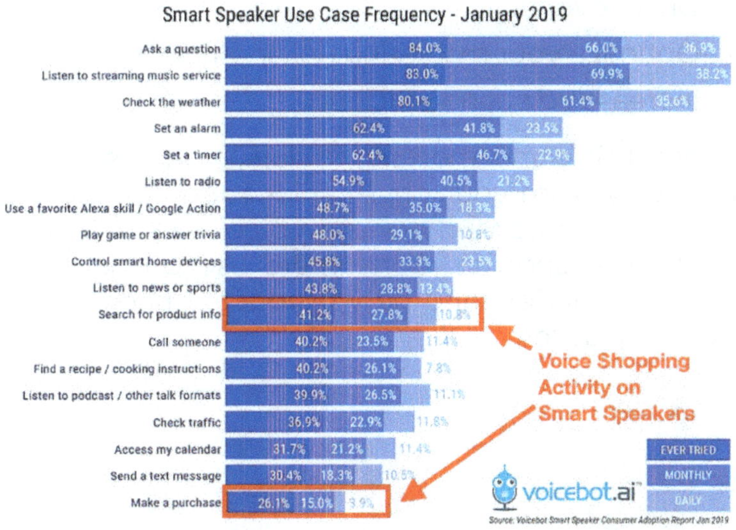

Source: Voicebot.ai, Smart Speaker Consumer Adoption Report – Jan 2019[131]

Say OK Google - Talk to Discovered Book – Smart Speaker Usage

Voice is working hard to deliver a better experience every single time. Until machines rule the world, the burden of building an incredible voice experience falls on our shoulders.

Intelligence Through Conversations

Voice is a rich source of data. For example, you can analyze conversations in real time and identify patterns associated with specific intents (questions) and outcomes (responses or actions).

The goal is to progress people further on their discovery, education, or customer experience. It doesn't matter if you are a consumer product, an insurance agent, or booking a residential quote for home improvements. Every brand has a voice utility.

Your brand can use these insights to:

- Drive revenue,
- Optimize your marketing dollar efficiency,
- Increase ad spend efficiency.

For those brick-and-mortar retailers, voice is not taking people away from your physical location; it's actually the opposite. When consumers use voice, 62% still choose a physical store shop in. Consumers use online search to discover and understand new products online to support their buying journey.

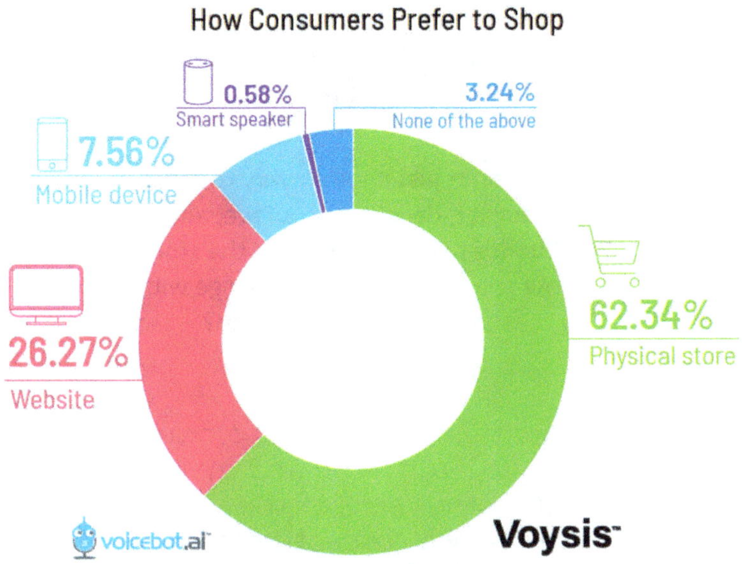

Source: Voicebot.ai, Voice Shopping Consumer Adoption Report[132]
Say OK Google - Talk to Discovered Book – Shoppers want in store

Shoppers would love to have more in-store integration with digital and voice.

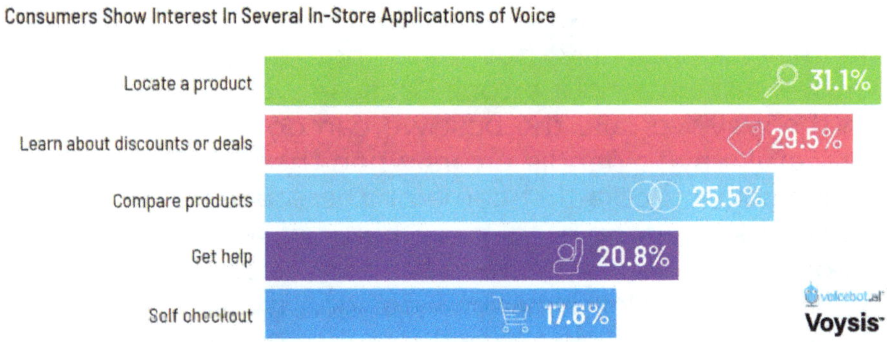

Source: Voicebot.ai, Voice Shopping Consumer Adoption Report[133]
Say OK Google - Talk to Discovered Book – Voice in store

Voice is not just another way to reach, educate, delight, encourage, and influence people to come to the store. How you can use voice to engage with shoppers in the store, too?

As people research and discover product information about your brand, we learn more and more about who the consumer is on the other side of the voice device. Every day on voice is a chance to capture the insight into the type of experience and relationships our consumers want to have with our brands.

Conversation IS the Experience

It's important to understand the conversation is what makes the experience extraordinary. As you create these voice interactions with your shoppers, your team may need to learn different skills about how to talk to people. It may sound silly but it is not easy to design a conversation without errors. Because we are so subjective in the way we talk, the best we can do is try to design a graceful way to handle errors when they occur. Much like when social media first came on the scene, there weren't positions or people to hire that just knew everything about social media. We're in the same situation right now with voice. Conversation design is a new thing. Conversational design experience is it a new thing. Voice user experience and customer experience is a territory that will have to be defined and tweaked over time.

You're not alone in this. My friends at RoboCopy across the pond in Amsterdam have created the first

Conversational training for Conversational Designers or companies that want to get their teams up to speed on Conversational Design. RoboCopy was an agency that pivoted to a training organization that is dedicated to helping people design better conversations. The course is available online to help teach people the basics around conversation design, error handling, and the intricacies that come along with designing better conversations with chatbots, voice assistants, and robots.

Check out Robocopy's Conversational Academy if you're interested in taking the training to become a certified Conversation Designer[134].

---

[134] *Say OK Google - Talk to Discovered Book – Robocopy Conversational Academy*

VOICE COMMERCE

When many people talk about voice, they talk about the money opportunity of voice but tend to lose sight of the conversation side of voice. The experience and conversation should definitely come before you begin to focus on commerce. While there is a commerce opportunity for many brands but that might not take place until stage two or three of your voice strategies.

Voice Commerce (vComm) is your brand's ability to sell on voice. The potential commerce opportunity for brands can be massive. The majority of voice predictions that have been made in the past have been blown out of the water. Since the adoption rate is so rapid, these are all just predictions based on what data we are just starting to gain access to.

Here's what you should know now:

1. Voice Commerce is estimated to be a $45[87]-$80[8] billion market by 2022[87] or 2023[8].
2. Amazon holiday season Q4 2018 voice shopping tripled[140].
3. The more users, the more usage, the better the experiences, the more sales!
4. Brands must move to an authentic (brand owned) customer experience.

---

140 *Say OK Google - Talk to Discovered Book – Amazon shopping triples*

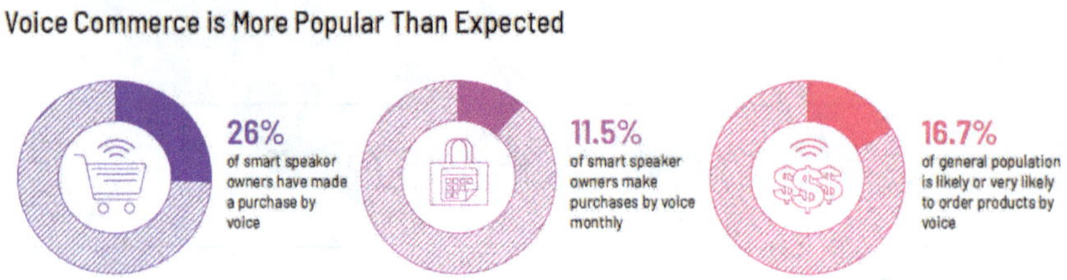

Source: Voicebot, US Smart Speaker Consumer Adoption 2018[141]

Say OK Google - Talk to Discovered Book – Voice Commerce is popular

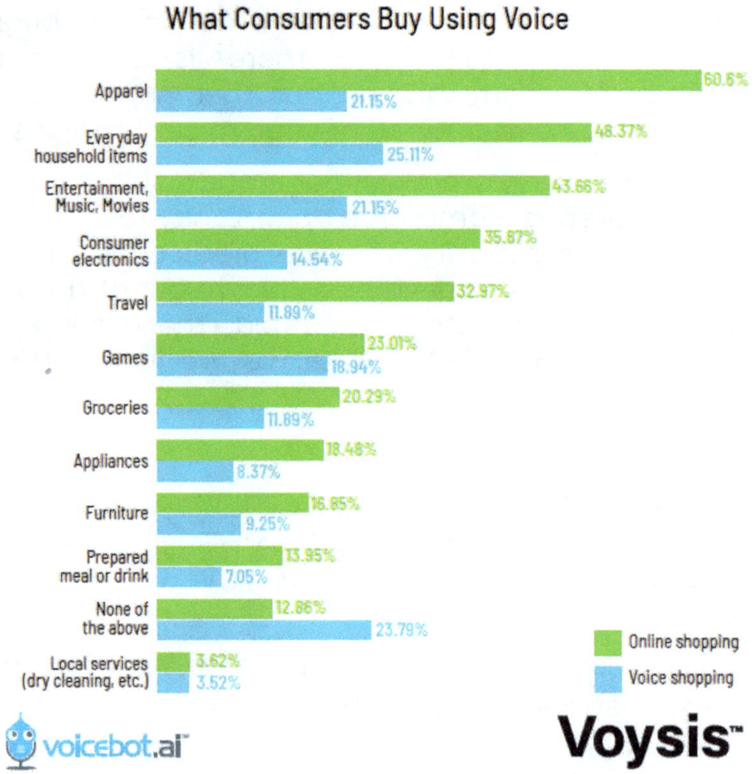

Source: Voicebot.ai, Voice Shopping Consumer Adoption Report[142]

Say OK Google - Talk to Discovered Book – What Consumers Buy

> It doesn't matter what you sell or what the age of your demographic is, they are all buying on voice.

Types of Shopper Order Using Voice

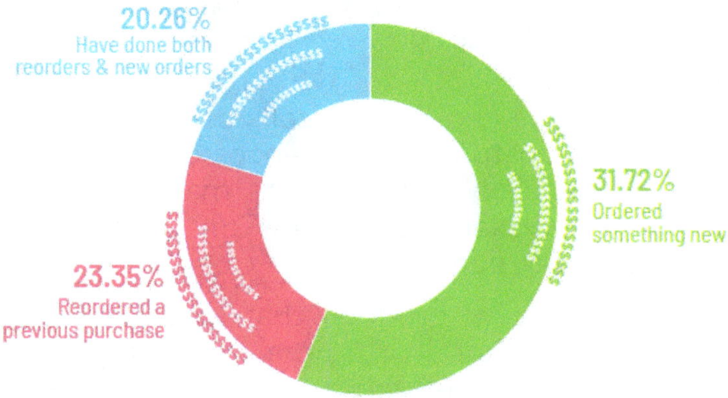

Source: Voicebot.ai, Voice Shopping Consumer Adoption Report[143]
Say OK Google - Talk to Discovered Book – Voice Shopping Orders

Understanding that voice is a new channel, it's incredible how many people are trying something brand-new that they hadn't discovered before through voice. Which today may be based off of just a mediocre experience and without many brands not even being represented on voice. Imagine the potential once many brands have built amazing voice customer experiences.

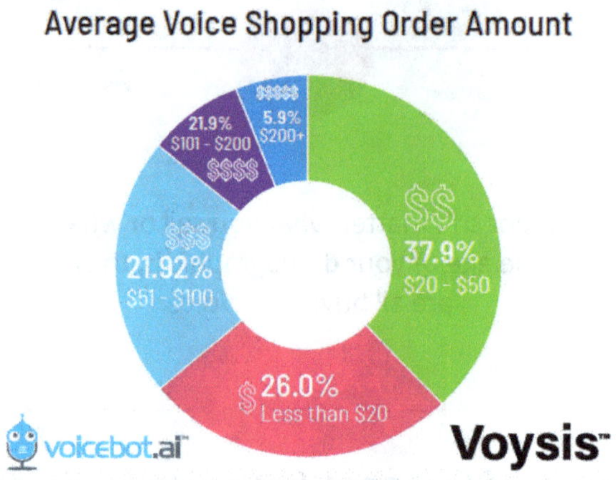

Source: Voicebot.ai, Voice Shopping Consumer Adoption Report[144]
Say OK Google - Talk to Discovered Book – Voice Order Amount

You can leverage voice to sell seemingly complex products. Voice customer experiences can be connected to How-to YouTube videos, DIY manuals, Customer Service guides, explanation videos on your website, or instructional audio recordings.

Imagine you have a product that you have spent a considerable amount of time creating beautiful instructional booklets delivered with every single product you sell. Yet your customer service center is always flooded with calls explaining step by step instructions on how to assemble your product. Much like my personal experience with assembling *any* piece of furniture that has 800 screws and so many pieces that they're labeled from A to ZZ. How amazing would it be if I just asked my Google assistant how to assemble a brand name piece of furniture? And my Google Assistant replied with the step by step instructions. This could replace the effort did the customer service center goes through to walk people through the steps to assemble. Your customer call center call traffic may go down allowing them to spend more quality time with customers on other valuable time. You're giving your customers the ability to truly be hands-free while assemble their furniture through a voice customer voice experience. This experience if presented through audio could be delivered on any smart speaker. Here's how this could work:

Me: *Hey Google, how do I put together a Hot Toddy Kids Bunk bed.*

Assistant: *It sounds like you may want help assembling your Hot Toddy Kids Bunk Bed. Do you have the name or model number of the bed?*

Me: *Yes. Model Super Awesome 1.*

Assistant: *Got it. I have the step by step instructions ready. Would you like me to walk you through the steps one by one or would you prefer to watch a video?*

Me: *Walk me through the steps please.*

Assistant: *No problem. Before we get started you will want to take everything out of the box and place the items on the floor with the stickers face up. There is also a box with screws and parts inside. You will need scissors to open the pouch of screws. When you have everything unpackaged and laid out, please say, "Hey Google, next step." and we can get started.*

Me: *Hey Google, next step.*

Assistant: *It sounds like you are all set to assemble your new bed. Here are the things I can help you with during your furniture assembly process:*

- If you would like me to repeat the instructions just say *"Repeat"*
- If you need to go back to a step just say "*Go back*"
- If you want to speak with a live person say, *"Help"*
- If you want to watch the video instead say, *"Video"*

Are you ready to start?

Me: *Yes*

Assistant: *Alrighty then. Let's do this! First, we will start by assembling the large base of the bed, which is marked with label A and 30 tiny screws...*

This is mimicking the exact interaction that happens on the phone with the customer service reps except we are trying to make it a bit better.

At the end of the experience, you can do several things. Ask them for feedback on the assembly experience. I love asking for feedback immediately following the experience. You can also do something fun with contests, photos, or posting with #momgoals on social channels. Have fun with it!

In addition to making furniture assembly not suck as much we are creating an open feedback loop with our customers. We may be able to learn where to improve our customer experience, instructions, or wording of instructions. When 300 people ask your assistant to Repeat a step, there must be something that is confusing in the process or the wording of the process.

Just as consumer behavior rapidly evolves today with search, buying journeys, and customer experiences, it will evolve on voice too. So, take this data for what it's worth right now but work hard to have an open feedback loop with your shoppers so you can always keep a pulse on what's happening.

What Consumers Like About Voice Shopping

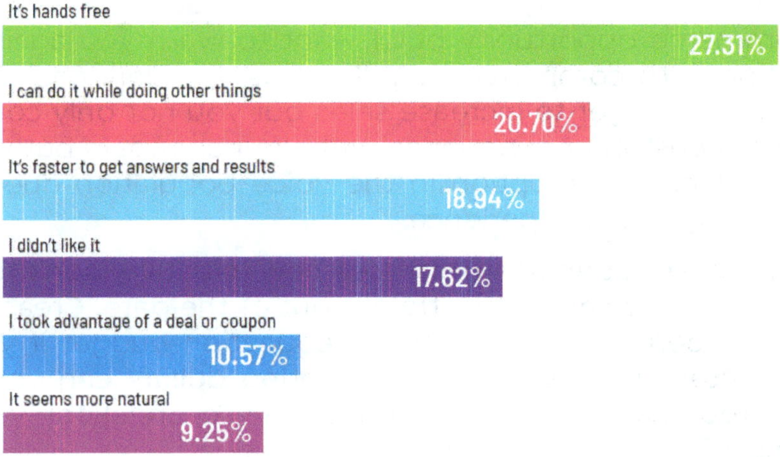

Source: Voicebot.ai, Voice Shopping Consumer Adoption Report[145]

Say OK Google - Talk to Discovered Book – I like it a lot!

What Consumers Do Not Like About Voice Shopping

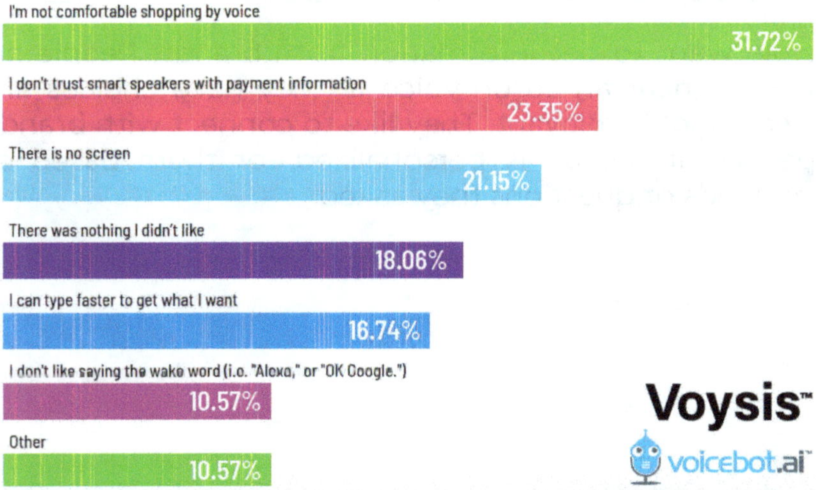

Source: Voicebot.ai, Voice Shopping Consumer Adoption Report[146]

Say OK Google - Talk to Discovered Book – I don't like it!

Purchases on Voice

People **are** buying on voice today. So, there is a vCommerce opportunity but I want to warn you against starting with commerce as THE focus. I understand that brands are eager to increase sales but you not only could ruin the customer experience with your shoppers but you could decrease adoption in the voice population due to delivering a poor experience.

If you must get an ROI from your new initiative, don't test it with a voice sales play straight out of the gate. Create a voice experience with a test or education budget if you can. Often times sales and marketing dollars can come with too many constraints for a new channel for your brand.

All of the data we've seen is pointing in the right direction. It's pretty amazing that so many have bought or would consider buying on voice.

Advertising on Voice

People want to get information from brands. People are willing to hear an ad on voice IF they have choices and they are highly relevant. They like to connect with brands, especially if the ad is personalized for them based on commands or questions they asked.

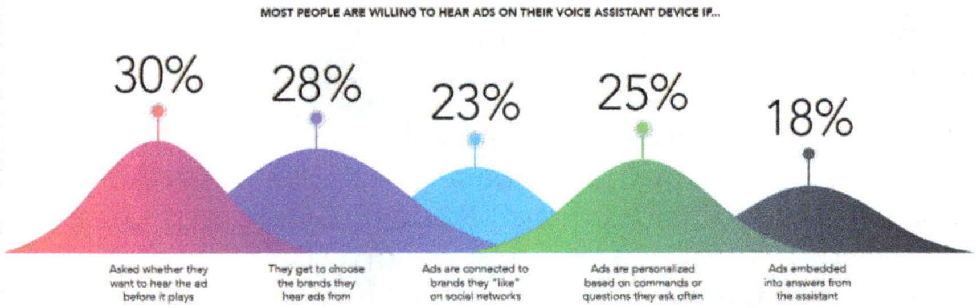

Source: Invoca, The Rise of Voice[147]

Say OK Google - Talk to Discovered Book – Shopper interaction

It's important that you understand the voice doesn't replace the human connection with our consumers.

- Voice can empower and educate your consumers.
- Voice should be a delightful experience.
- Voice experiences should be memorable and share-worthy.

Many brands are taking their ads to the next level using Artificial Intelligence (AI). Consumers are becoming more aware of AI and becoming more comfortable with the idea. In fact, 72% of Millennials believe that brands can use technology, like AI to accurately predict what they will want to buy[148].

How shoppers respond to AI completely depends on their values. Baby Boomers value customer service, they value people having conversations with them. Millennials on the other than think it is possible to build in emotional intelligence enough to make the experience desirable. How you embrace AI in your brand has too many variables to go into but I encourage you to check out the reports.

Adobe & Invoca - Emotions Wins: What Customers Expect in the Age of AI. This report is focused on the data around

---

[148] *Say OK Google - Talk to Discovered Book – Millenials AI*

the emotions, psychology and beliefs from Millennials to Boomers[149].

To read a bit deeper on using AI for to maximize your visibility with your ads, increase your Return on Ad Spend (ROAS) and to reduce ad fraud. Check out Juniper's Whitepaper (free) or Research report The Impact of AI for Digital Advertisers[150].

Brands that are looking to future-proof their marketing are embracing innovation to disrupt and lead their category. If domination is not your thing, voice can still be used to just get noticed in a distracted digital consumer world.

---

[149] *Say OK Google - Talk to Discovered Book – Emotions Win*

[150] *Say OK Google - Talk to Discovered Book – Impact of AI*

VOICE USE CASES

Voice gives your brand ways to create a memorable shopping experience. The experience is becoming a new focus that is equally important as being discovered in the first place. We are relentless when we have a bad experience. One in three people will walk away from a brand if they have a bad experience[155]. Most people share poor experiences more often than wonderful experiences. It is a must in today's business climate to always look for ways to improve the experience.

A positive shopping experience can mean deeper loyalty, greater trust, and more money spent. On average, 80% of consumers who have shopped using their voice assistant are satisfied, and as a result[156]:

- 39% shared their positive experiences with friends and family
- 39% shopped again with the same retailer
- 36% have a more favorable opinion of the retailer
- 24% spent more money with the retailer

[155] *Say OK Google - Talk to Discovered Book – Experience is Everything*

[156] *Say OK Google - Talk to Discovered Book – Positive Voice Experiences*

Yet, lack of trust is still palpable[157]. One out of every four consumers would not consider shopping through their voice assistant now or in the future:

- 46% said "I don't trust my voice assistant to correctly interpret and process my order."
- 45% said "I don't trust or feel comfortable sending payment through my voice assistant."

We do have some idea what shoppers appear to be most excited about with their voice experiences.

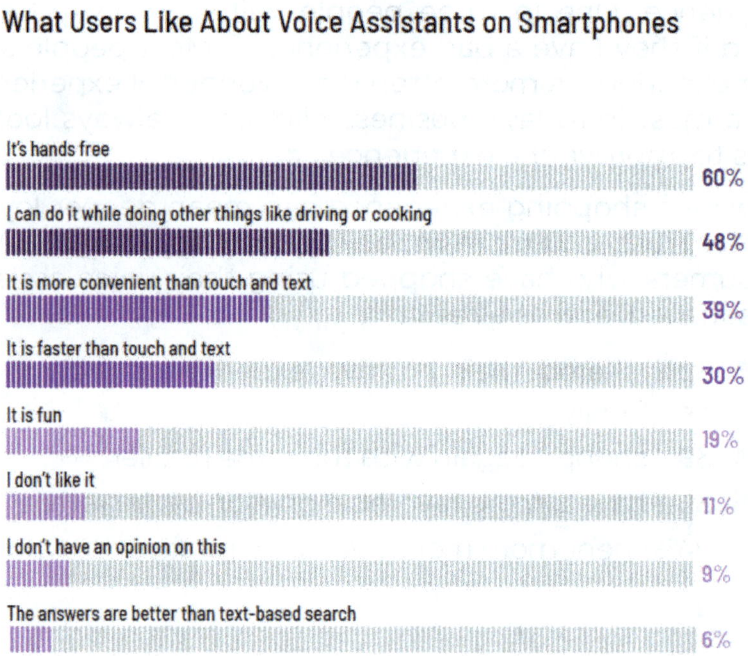

Source: Voicebot.ai - Voice Assistant Consumer Adoption Report 2018[158]

Say OK Google - Talk to Discovered Book –Like about Voice Experiences

---

[157] *Say OK Google - Talk to Discovered Book – Lack of Voice Trust*

When building voice experiences for smartphones, keep it top of mind how important hands free and great conversational design is to the shopper. The top four responses require the experience to be completely hands free. Those are different design challenges than what we typically have to deal with for mobile or web design.

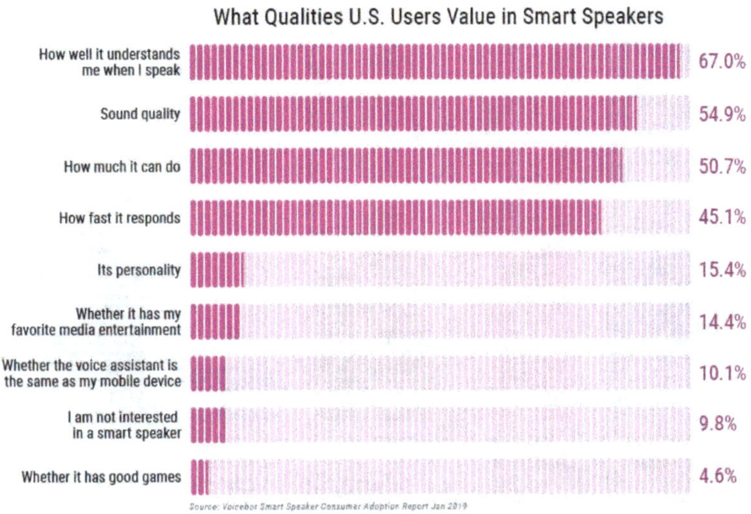

Source: Voicebot.ai - Voice Assistant Consumer Adoption Report 2018[159]

Say OK Google - Talk to Discovered Book – Quality Voice Experience

Some of these examples aren't as focused on hands free because smart speakers have never been handheld whereas the phones are completely designed to be handheld. Can you design one great experience that will satisfy everyone? You should try. You may not get them all the first round but that's to be expected. Choose the primary experiential, emotional, or conversational goal and build that utility the best you can. You can always build on to it and make it a stronger use case.

Since voice is a new behavior, we are still figuring out how to make it viral and referable. Think of ways that we can make it easier to share for our friends to discover? Use and adoption will continue to climb as we build amazing voice experiences.

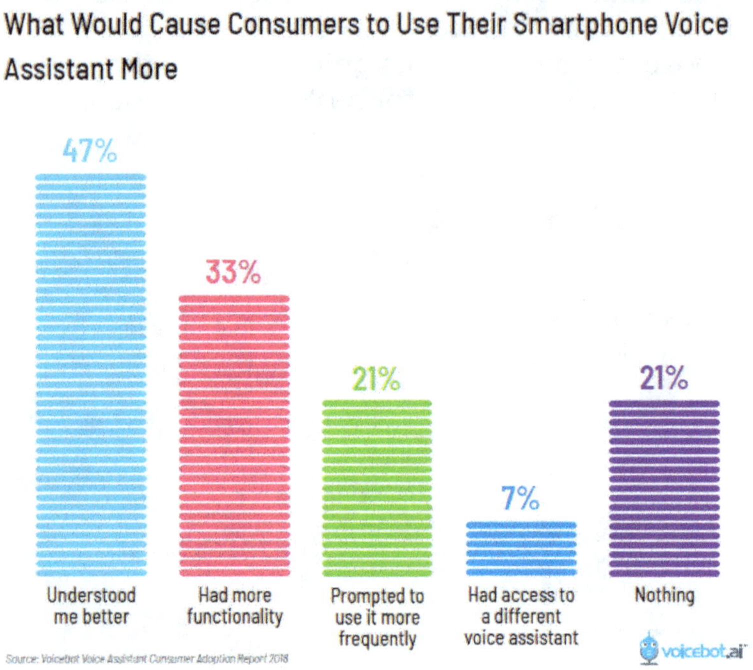

Source: Voicebot.ai - Voice Assistant Consumer Adoption Report 2018[160]

Say OK Google - Talk to Discovered Book – Why Use Voice More

Brand Voice Use Cases

The following examples highlight how voice can be used effectively for various brands.

1) Campbells - Conversations Transformed an Organization

Challenge: How to combat steadily declining sales and diminishing relevance.

Solution: Reimagine the company's entire approach to digital.

Validated Assumptions: Across all 22 audience segments, dinner was consistently the biggest shopper problem.

Hypothesis: Recipes were a huge driver of sales. Dinner recipes had four times more traffic than all other pages combined but they couldn't attribute sales uplift to recipes.

Test: Create a content hub with a laser focus to solve dinner.

Results:

- **37% increase in new household penetration** - Drove new customers and brand switchers to Campbells cooking brands.
- **36-63% increase in existing household brand spending** - Across the portfolio of products

2) Tide - Untapped Consumer Insights Fueled Product Innovation

Challenge: How to reinforce the brand's position as the "go-to-stain-solver."

Solution: Create a voice experience around the "know" moments they should own.

Hypothesis: When a stain strikes, shoppers have their hands full, and dirty, they need fast, reliable answers in a completely hands-free experience.

Test:

- Alexa voice skill with more than 200 stain types with step-by-step instructions.
- Give the brand visibility to Alexa user's email by linking to Amazon account.
- Give a visual experience when possible.

Results:

- Gave brand visibility to hundreds of users a day.
- Providing informational assistance translated into strong emotional resonance.
- Became an insight engine into brand new consumer insights.
- Increased brand affinity.
- Elevated the skill to unbranded queries (ie when no one was asking for "Tide").

3) Nike - ~~Mic~~ Shoe- Drop Moments

Challenge: Do something no other brand had done. LIVE Shoe Drop NBA broadcast of the L.A. Lakers vs. Boston Celtics game on TNT (with more than 2 million viewers).

Test: Collaborative approach between brand teams, creative agency, and voice partner to offer a LIVE Shoe Drop that was only offered through a voice-activated offer. Google Search activated only - not Alexa.

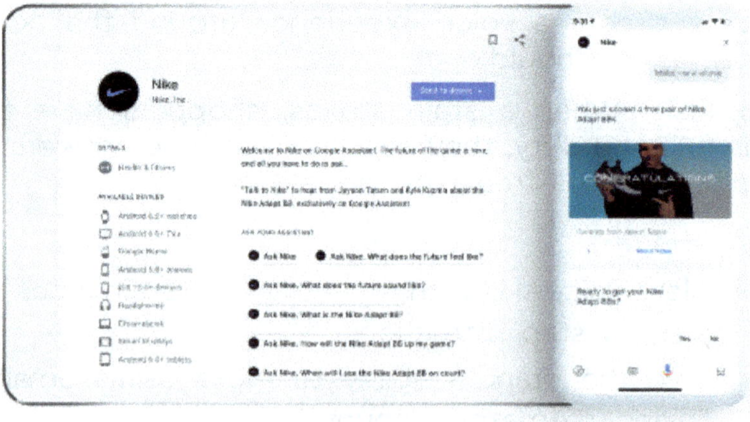

Image Source: Nike Shoe Drop[161]

Say OK Google - Talk to Discovered Book – Nike Voice UX

Results:

- Let's just say that it blew estimates out of the water.
- Now, Nike is working on how to use voice to elevate their aggressive growth to their new focus of a $250B direct-to-consumer channel[18].

There are also several use cases where voice was able to create a new customer experience behavior. Headspace, the mediation app was able to create a new voice engagement experience to meditate through voice experiences.

Results:

- Within 60 days, Headspace reached the same number of users that it took 40 months to reach on mobile.
- 90% return rate - Almost everyone returned for another session.

aLoft was able to create new guest experiences by offering guest assistance through voice through in room smart speakers.

Results:

- Pilot increased guest engagement by 37% (money maker).
- Diverted 4,000 basic commands away from the front desk (cost saver).

Now, Marriott is making a significant investment into expanding internal infrastructure and systems across multiple brands and properties to incorporate voice into its global footprint.

Building for Retention

When designing your voice skill, it is important to understand the frequency versus the utility. A voice application that may be used frequently could be an alarm clock or the weather. We might set a timer every night when we prepare dinner. Or we might send an alarm or reminder to perform a certain task. Many of us check the weather daily. We may not personally care who provides us the information on the weather. The frequency is very high when it comes to daily mundane informational tasks.

Ideally, we want a voice experience that has high utility and high frequency, which could potentially pose a huge design challenge. If we are building a voice experience to solve a one-time problem, then the shopper doesn't have a reason to visit the voice experience again. The frequency could be over after the first interaction. We want to build a voice conversation that gives shoppers a reason to come back. A perfect example with Campbell's Soup what's for dinner? That is a problem in my house on a daily basis. Helping me plan my dinner is something that has high utility and high frequency for me and my family.

Voice is like getting a do-over in marketing. We've all been there when we think of something wittier or funnier to say after the fact. Similarly if we would have sent an email marketing campaign and we realized we forgot the coupon code *after* we hit the send button.

Voice can be a continuation of a conversation. It can be a way to tell people about your brand switching to all natural ingredients, building a community, and getting feedback to drive your own product's innovation.

When you're building a new voice experience, consider your retention strategy for a longer term reward. If you can build in a high utility WITH a high frequency, you nailed it. You can be the President of the Pat-Yourself-on-the-Back club again.

Voice Landscape

Today, there are over 80,000 Alexa skills (voice experiences) but there are only a small percentage of skills that are useful and valuable.

Source: Alexa, AskMarvee.com[162]

Say OK Google - Talk to Discovered Book – Voice Uses by Age

You can create a voice experience for people that are 3 to 93. Your vision of what voice can do may be possible as long as you are mindful of the skill level, expectation, and capacity of having a conversation (ie toddlers learning to speak and may not know how to answer questions).

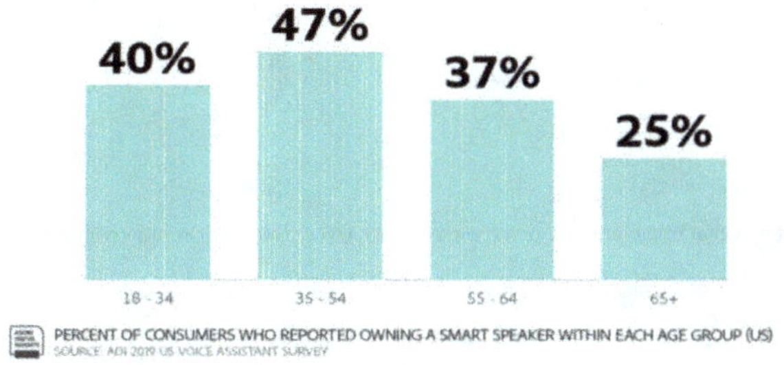

Source: Adobe Insight 2019[163]

Say OK Google - Talk to Discovered Book – Smart Speaker Demographics

Even though adoption is driven by the younger demographics, the frequency and usage is higher among the older demographics. Don't dismiss any particular age group on voice. They are all there! Imagine the friction points in your customer experience and make them better with an incredible voice customer experience.

VOICE STRATEGY

As agencies, specialists, and brands learn more about the best use case for voice, our strategies and approaches will evolve to improve. However, there are a couple nuggets to share that I hope will reduce any bumps on your voice journey.

Executive Buy-in

It is critical to get buy-in at the CxO level. The executive leadership team has to be bought in to the vision. Executives have the most to gain *and* the most to lose. The leadership team will help support the rest of the team to ensure they have the right consultants, agencies, skills in house, budget, and messaging to set expectations of voice for the rest of the organization.

Top Voice Application Initiatives for Businesses

Source: Adobe Insights[170]

Say OK Google - Talk to Discovered Book – Top Voice Objectives

When I see this data, I cringe. Voice should be treated as a crawl, walk, run approach. Enable customer purchases and enable repeat purchases and renewals is running before you learn to crawl and walk. The risk to our brands with this approach is coming off too sales-y before your voice experience has built rapport and earned our shoppers trust, which can have a ripple effect on the voice channel as a whole.

Be Flexible with the Process

Voice is extremely flexible but filled with constraints. Be flexible with the process and with your ideas. It is a process that should be approached in phases. Each phase your team will learn, improve their skills, and you can pivot accordingly.

We favor the crawl - walk - run process:

<u>Crawl - Start and Learn</u>

This is where you just get started. Ideate, and agree on a use case to begin with. Determine what your hypothesis is and create the experience. There should not be an expectation of any ROI. No KPIs at this point either. This is where you start to CREATE a baseline. You will have no baseline before you start and other research and data may or may not be relevant to your brand or your customers.

<u>Walk - Lessons Learned</u>

Collect the insights of what happened with the launch of the voice experience. Did the shoppers behave as you expected them to? Were your hypothesis or assumptions correct? What did you learn? What can your team do to improve and optimize the experience? Begin to think about discoverability. What can we do to increase visibility and awareness of the voice experience organically?

Run - Integration

Now your team should have a fundamental understanding of the voice experience's value and how to integrate it into your digital ecosystem. Are their packaging opportunities to promote and market engagement? Are their retail activations where you can talk to shoppers and show them the skill? Instead of demos and sampling, some brands have used their retailer in-store activations to show the voice experience and get feedback from shoppers. You may also begin to think about where, when, and how to advertise and promote the voice experiences.

Collaboration

Voice should be a collaborative effort. The most successful voice use cases come from organizations that share a culture of collaboration. Teams that work in silos tend to present more challenges than collaborative environments. Voice strategies executed well include multiple teams:

- Customer Service
- Social Media
- User Experience/ Design
- Market Data/ Research/ Insight
- Web/ Search/ Mobile
- Marketing/ Branding
- Creative/ Content/ Copy
- Sales/ Channels
- Engineering

All teams may not be necessary for the entire project but in most cases each team has valuable insight that could make the voice experience better for the shopper. At a minimum, Chief Experience Officers should be aware and engaged in the critical strategy phase of the project and apprised of progress in case they need to loop in the necessary team members.

Team

Since voice is a fairly new platform, most companies may not have the team in house to design and get off on the right foot, just as social media was new and created new problems, solutions, positions, and eventually new degrees. You may already have people on your team that would embrace and excel with voice or you may need to bring on new team members.

Short-Term Campaigns

Voice is not a transient competency. There have been voice experiences created around campaigns to support a targeted initiative. Voice pilots have been created around a campaign but it is not straightforward as a social media, media buy, or retail activation. We have taken years to master the planning, coordination, and execution of those campaigns and voice doesn't drop into campaigns as easily.

Again, the power of voice is in search, gathering intelligence, and creating an experience that blows your competition out of the water while building brand affinity with millions of people. That takes time and may need to fall under a testing budget versus a marketing play.

Create Future Experiences

Imagine new experiences. Create new behaviors.

Don't just build something cool,
build a truly transformative experience.

Imagine what the experience could be by looking through a future lens, not what you know it to be today. Voice has positive transformational effects.

When cars were designed, planners focused heavily on building broader streets and highways. Dirt roads would no longer due and many were only big enough to handle one car travelling one direction, not big enough for two cars. Logically, highways was the only problem to focus on. What we missed were the suburbs. We didn't think about housing, schools, gas stations, grocery stores, and restaurants. A future problem was thinking beyond the immediate problem and understanding what new problems could arise or what new behaviors could happen. This brainstorming and thought process may be different from what most of us are used to doing but it is super fun to design for the future that doesn't yet exist.

Voice and...

Voice is not a replacement for what you are doing right now, meaning you are not going to stop social media and just do voice. You should stop SEO for desktop and mobile search and only focus on voice search. Voice is a *compliment* to what you may already have in place today. There has been great success around customer service, answering questions that are common around gifts, returns, locations, etc. You may have experiences that may exist on other channels or content that would be relevant and useful in a different format. You can use voice to make it easier to find a how-to video, instructions on how to perform a return, or how to get points for referring new customers. Anyone can find a great use case but it is key to verify that the use case is desired by your customers and shoppers before you build otherwise you risk wasting time or money.

I would recommend picking up the book Sprint, How to Solve Big Problems and Test New Ideas in Just Five Days by Jake Knapp[171]. I love this approach when testing and validating ideas rapidly. The approach has been used by countless companies and is also been coined by Google as the Google Design Sprint since it is ingrained into their process and the process their startup venture funded companies go through. It is a super quick read and should be read by anyone on your team that will be a part of this project.

New Challenges

Voice can be incredibly entertaining. You can create story-based experiences similar to Dunkirk, Jurassic World, or Kung Fu Panda. You can leverage brand influencers. But you may have new challenges in who owns the audio content. This is a different play than YouTube videos, blog posts, or one-time Instagram posts. Contracts may not exist. Licensing structures may have to be created but it can totally be handled.

Be aware of new risks with your experience. Could someone steal your experience idea and build it, right now, yes. We didn't have voice experiences to protect in the past. If you build your voice customer experiences with your authentic brand voice, that only you have, your competition will fail because they won't be able to mimic your voice well, at least not for long.

---

[171] *Say OK Google - Talk to Discovered Book – Sprint Book*

Voice Design Considerations

Pick One Problem

It is always hard to stay focused on just one thing, but when designing your voice experience, it is important to start small first. If you are narrowly focused on one problem, it helps your team stay laser-focused on that problem. Imagine how quickly a conversation could get off track...

The What's for Dinner Voice Skill was launched in 2015 by Campbells Soup (built by Rain Agency). The team asked the question, "what moves the needle?" The voice strategy was rooted in the problem: **How do you solve dinner?** Dinner moves Campbells business. Before voice, Campbells has the hypothesis that recipes contributed to sales but they didn't have definitive data that proved this. Because of voice, Campbells now know that recipes *do* impact sales.

Hit Conversational Gold Mines

Regardless of the maturity of your data experience, this is a chance to level up your data game. Take some time to mine conversations in your organization. Everyone that has touchpoints with your customers has a unique perspective and data points that may be conversational gold in your voice experience.

Here are a few places that you can look for conversational gold:

- Customer Service Call Logs
- Customer Service Chat Logs
- Customer Service Knowledge Base (Help desk, ticket systems)

- Social Media Channel
- Technical Support or Engineering
- Product Management
- Data, Knowledge Management or Customer Insight Teams
- Sales (Inside, Outside, Partner, Distribution Channels, ALL sales teams)
- Marketing
- And anyone else that touches a customer

What is their customer experience like? What are they conversations like? You want to understand what conversations are happening with the customers across these various customer experiences. Understanding everyone's unique perspective not only gives you a better world view of your brand but it gives you an opportunity to look for patterns and gaps in the data. This can help you create a better voice experience than with just your team alone.

Don't Skip Dinner

It's easy to get so excited about an incredible product that we ask for the sale too early. Since voice is a new channel with a fair share of privacy issues, trust becomes your barrier. Some people already trust voice and will purchase. But don't ask your dream girl out to dinner and go straight to dessert and skip all the fun that leads up to the sweet stuff. That's creepy and you might as well just ask her if she wants to go back to your place as soon as she sits in the car. Not cool.

Design Constraints

Voice offers a wonderful opportunity with freedom to build a future-proof experience. But you may be challenged with creating something amazing with one hand tied behind your back. Voice has a fair share of constraints. Imagine you're building a car while you are still driving it. It certainly could be challenging.

Virality, Community, Loops

It's still too early to tell if the virality lies within the experience itself or is there a viral loop outside of the platform or the experience. As brands build experiences on voice, is there a way to connect people through community and loops? Pinterest offers easy-to-share boards to loop people into an experience. Facebook and LinkedIn build communities through groups. What is that for voice? It's too early to tell for sure.

One thing we do know is that people do not leave reviews on voice like they do on other platforms. If you don't have a screen, it's not easy to navigate to the review to leave one. If you do have a screen, most likely, you have other more important things to deal with, so it just doesn't happen often.

Do you know what people do leave reviews (and some really long reviews) about? Bad voice experiences. I know, it's our world. Most people have good intentions when leaving reviews, even poor ones, to save someone else from the hassle they personally experienced.

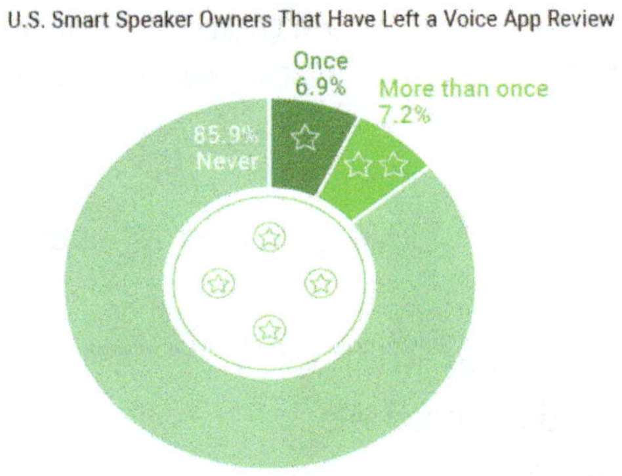

Source: Voicebot.ai, Smart Speaker Consumer Adoption Report 2019[172]
Say OK Google - Talk to Discovered Book – Consumer Voice Reviews

Design Requirements

When designing voice experiences, you must go deeper than web design. We should consider emotional and conversational requirements, in addition to any technical or engineering requirements. Use cases and design requirements may change between brands, even at the same company. Different product, different problems.

Consider Ecosystems

Incorporating your brand's ecosystems, technical systems, and data will help the team understand how to integrate and automate the voice data. Take customer service calls as an example; often 80% of customer service calls are about a few questions. We can create an API that connects to the customer service chat log system, knowledge base, or FAQ. If you launch a new product category, you may have new questions, you can create an automation process. If a question is asked 20 times, it qualifies for a knowledge base and FAQ worthy question. If that happens, that question can automatically feed your voice experience.

Spend Time on Errors

A lot of time. Errors can make for a voice experience disaster. It is almost as important to design for errors and mistakes as it is for the conversational experience itself.

Discoverability

Voice is a channel. Every channel struggles to gain visibility:

- Websites - eCommerce
- Social Media Channels
- Promos/ Offers/ Campaigns
- Mobile Apps

Voice is much like other channels and discoverability is no different. There is a page that you can search for Alexa Skills and Google Actions but whoever goes there, besides me and techie developer folks? Let's just assume that shoppers are not searching for a voice experience that can improve their lives. You have to be found.

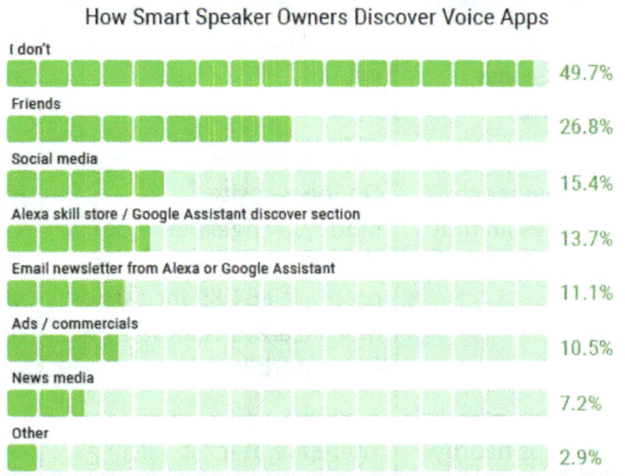

Source: Voicebot.ai, Smart Speaker Consumer Adoption Report 2019[173]
Say OK Google - Talk to Discovered Book – Voice Discovery

The good news is there is hope. When we talked about Schema and how it is the foundation of search, we are also seeing that Schema is important to discoverability on Google. Actions by Google are super slick and is built from an experiential standpoint across platforms, devices, and channels. I believe that every single Google interface is running with machine learning, probably neural machine learning behind it, so it can learn how to be better for you as you use them.

An incredible agency Rabbit and Pork, which is a subsidiary of Roast out of the United Kingdom has the most advanced understanding of how voice search happens on Google. Here are the elements that they found matter the most (right now) for voice search discoverability. This data is available by dozens of industries on their website[174].

Voice Search Results Data

Answer Type	Example Key Phrase	Example Response	Source for Answer
No Response	small business loans	Sorry, I can't help with that yet.	No answer available.
Answer	how much does an mot cost	On the website moneysavingexpert. com, they say: The maximum test costs are £54.85 for cars or motor caravans and £29.65 for motorbikes.	Featured snippets answer boxes of google web results
Answer - Location Result (3 listings)	pubs nearby	There are at least 3 listings. The 1st one is: O'Neill's Kings Cross, on 73-77 Euston Rd in London. You can say: directions, call, details, or next.	Google My Business listings
Answer - News Playback	todays world news	"Would start to play news from a 3rd party"	Built into the Google Assistant
Answer - Knowledge Graph	best accounting software	Software frequently mentioned on the web include: QuickBooks, Microsoft Dynamics GP, SAP ERP, and others.	Google's Knowledge Panel

[174] *Say OK Google - Talk to Discovered Book – Voice Search Results*

Answer Type	Example Key Phrase	Example Response	Source for Answer
Answer - Location Result (3 listings) - Old Style	toy donations	I found a few places. The 1st one is The Toy Project at 99 Junction Rd in London. The 2nd one is Toy House at 92 St Paul's Way in London. The 3rd one is Lewisham Toy Library at 46, Lewisham Shopping Centre, Molesworth St in London.	Google My Business listings
Answer - Location Result (1 listing)	motor finance	MotoNovo Finance is on 1 Central Square in Cardiff. You can say: directions or call.	Google My Business listings
Answer - Action prompt	how to make a white Russian	Okay. For that, you might like tender. Want to give them a try?	Implicit Invocation of an Assistant Action
Answer - Link on Google Home app	house for sale in Sheffield	I don't have an exact answer, but on rightmove.co.uk, I found a page called Properties for sale in Sheffield. If you want to read more, follow the link I just sent to your phone.	Google My Business listings
Answer - Location Result (2 listings)	Nissan finance	There are at least 2 listings. The 1st one is: Nissan Finance Ltd, on Rivers Office Park, Denham Way in Rickmansworth. You can say: directions, call, or next.	Google My Business listings
Answer - Definition	what is a accumulator	accumulator. a person or thing that accumulates something.	Google's Knowledge Panel

Answer Type	Example Key Phrase	Example Response	Source for Answer
Answer - Action Reminder	when's my mot up	I couldn't find anything related to "mot up"	Built into the Google Assistant
Answer - Location Result (3 listings)	pubs nearby	There are at least 3 listings. The 1st one is: O'Neill's Kings Cross, on 73-77 Euston Rd in London. You can say: directions, call, details, or next.	Google My Business listings
Answer - News Playback	todays world news	"Would start to play news from a 3rd party"	Built into the Google Assistant
Answer - Knowledge Graph	best accounting software	Software frequently mentioned on the web include: QuickBooks, Microsoft Dynamics GP, SAP ERP, and others.	Google's Knowledge Panel
Answer - Location Result (3 listings) - Old Style	toy donations	I found a few places. The 1st one is The Toy Project at 99 Junction Rd in London. The 2nd one is Toy House at 92 St Paul's Way in London. The 3rd one is Lewisham Toy Library at 46, Lewisham Shopping Centre, Molesworth St in London.	Google My Business listings
Answer - Location Result (1 listing)	motor finance	MotoNovo Finance is on 1 Central Square in Cardiff. You can say: directions or call.	Google My Business listings

Answer Type	Example Key Phrase	Example Response	Source for Answer
Answer - Action prompt	how to make a white Russian	Okay. For that, you might like tender. Want to give them a try?	Implicit Invocation of an Assistant Action
Answer - Link on Google Home app	house for sale in Sheffield	I don't have an exact answer, but on rightmove.co.uk, I found a page called Properties for sale in Sheffield. If you want to read more, follow the link I just sent to your phone.	Google My Business listings
Answer - Location Result (2 listings)	Nissan finance	There are at least 2 listings. The 1st one is: Nissan Finance Ltd, on Rivers Office Park, Denham Way in Rickmansworth. You can say: directions, call, or next.	Google My Business listings
Answer - Definition	what is an accumulator	Accumulator. a person or thing that accumulates something.	Google's Knowledge Panel
Answer - Action Reminder	when's my mot up	I couldn't find anything related to "mot up"	Built into the Google Assistant

Answer Type	Example Key Phrase	Example Response	Source for Answer
Short ABR & Link to App	gluten free alcohol	"I found 6 on the website glutenfreesurvivalguide.org. Here are the first 4. Avoid beer unless it is specifically brewed to be gluten-free., Rum, tequila, and potato vodka are gluten-free., Whiskey and bourbon are not universally accepted as gluten-free, so proceed with caution., and finally, Wine is typically gluten-free and safe to drink.	Featured snippets ABRs on Google Web results
GMB Opening Times	Hotels open near me	"Central Hotel London is open until 00:00 on Tuesday."	Google My Business Listings
Morning Routine	what's going on near me today	Changes depending on device settings	Google Assistant
Recipe Action	cocktail recipes	"Okay. I've got a recipe called Margarita from Jamie Oliver. Does that sound good?"	Website Recipe Schema
Similar Question	which wine is best for you	"I'm not sure, but I can tell you the answer to a similar question:	Google Assistant

Source: Roast, Rabbit and Pork Voice Search Results Report, A deep dive into verticals[174]

Say OK Google - Talk to Discovered Book – Voice Search Results

Google Assistant Strategies

If you do Schema well AND leverage other critical Google recommendations on your brand site and online profile (as seen in the table above), then the chances are better for you with Google Action discoverability.

Here are a few key strategies to start:

- Treat Google Channels as a Marketing Channel to optimize your online presence for voice
- Create a Knowledge Graph Strategy (to get one or make it better)
- Setup a Local Products Inventory feed[175] so Google can easily find your inventory and direct people to it. This is key to getting ranked locally, which is major for "Where to Purchase" queries.
- Claim, setup or optimize your Google My Business Local Business profile.
- Optimize your website content for Featured Snippets (Position 0 or Answer Box)
- Create a relevant, current FAQ page based on conversational data.
- Answer questions in a list answer format, if possible. Otherwise keep answers to between 29 and 60 words.

Alexa Strategies

Amazon is a tough shell to crack since they are like an overly protective parent when it comes to customer data and insight. But here are a few things to consider if you are interested in creating an Alexa voice experience:

---

[175] *Say OK Google - Talk to Discovered Book – Product Inventory Feed*

- If you sell products on Amazon, work your tails off to get your products marked "Amazon's Choice"[176]
- Confirm the first 2-3 sentences of your Wikipedia page is accurate and sounds delightful if read by Alexa. If not edit it!
- Create or optimize your Yelp profile which is key for Alexa local searches
- Keep an eye for the release of Alexa Conversations. Limited access available in Summer 2019 for selected Developers. Must apply to be considered. Alexa conversations will be useful to help shoppers find the right selection based on a conversation between Alexa and the shopper.

Optimize for Voice

This is still a process of discovery and learning even for our teams, which are immersed in this world every day. Be patient with the process and respect the challenge your team will have finding answers to problems. It's just the nature of innovation and emerging technology.

Here are a couple of optimization strategies to get started:

- View your brand through a Google Lens. Google has several channels to use (for free) to help your brand get discovered. Is your brand found on them?
    - Google Express
    - Google My Business (GMB)
    - Google Maps (part of GMB)
    - Local Product Inventory Feed
    - Actions by Google (Voice Actions or Apps)
    - Leverage ImplicitInvocation

---

[176] *Say OK Google - Talk to Discovered Book – Amazon's Choice*

- Start using Schema Markup. There is long-term value in this since desktop and mobile search continues to climb, this will help with all search channels.
- Optimize third party pages – Wikipedia, Yelp, GetHuman
- Amazon
  - Strive for Amazon's Choice for your product pages
  - Optimize Amazon Product page for SEO
  - Create a valuable Alexa skills – Start small
  - Leverage CanFulfillIntentRequest (CFIR)
- Optimize web content for questions
  - Create a FAQ based on conversational data
  - Answer 29 words that can be read within 12 seconds
  - Be concise, direct, and brief. Answer the question immediately. Fluff later.
  - Answer What, How, Where, When, and Who
- Optimize Video Content
  - Apply Schema to your How To's videos on YouTube. See the template in Resources section of the DiscoveredBook website[64].
  - Connect your Alexa Skill to your How To's videos too.
- Make it easy to find a human. Robots can be fun and cool but frustrating as heck if you need to find a person.
  - Explain in your voice experience how to find help or reach a live person. Shoppers will love you for it.

Possible Discoverability Advantages

There may be two discoverability advantages open to brands right now. The Voice platform trying to get as many questions as possible answered with the best answer this is an amazing opportunity for Brands to take advantage of. There are specific actions that can be taken with your voice experience today that are wide open to anyone armed with the right information. My prediction is this window is closing by the day.

Here's an example, when a shopper asks a question about the problem they're trying to solve how they asked the question may be different from person to person.

A friend of mine, Jennifer Lopez, has a company that helps families get their time back by providing done for you household services which are the tasks that no one wants to do, like grocery shopping, meal prep, home organization, and laundry. Her company is called Assistant Pro[177] and she could have people ask hundreds of questions (and problems) that she solves. Here are a couple of questions that people may ask:

- Home organizers near me
- How much do house organizers cost?
- Are home assistants expensive in Florida?
- How much does laundry service cost?
- Can I hire someone to buy my groceries & food prep?
- How to declutter my home
- How to keep my kid's room clean
- Quick ways for meal prep
- How to do meal prep fast

---

[177] *Say OK Google - Talk to Discovered Book – Assistant Pro Rocks*

- Weekly meal plans, templates or checklists
- How to create healthy meal plans?

All of these problems can be solved by Assistant Pro. If I tell Google when you see these questions, I can answer them on my website, they could send hundreds of the right people with the problem that only your brand solves so well, directly to your site.

Here's how the scenario could play out:

Shopper: *How much does laundry service cost?*

Google Assistant: *Laundry service costs vary based on how much laundry you have on a weekly basis and whether or not you want at home, out of home, or delivery service. It looks like Assistant Pro has additional information about how to find affordable laundry service, would you like to see/ read/ hear/ watch more?*

Shopper: *Yes, please*!

BOOM - In Assistant Pro's world!

As a part of building the voice customer experience you tell Google, these 500 questions would be answered with this one webpage. This could be a FAQ page that talks all about how you can get your life back by hiring someone to help with these things that take all weekend away from your family. What I love about what Jennifer is doing is she has a mission to make this affordable to middle-income families and she is committed to her mission. She is SUPER reasonable and most people don't even realize these services are as affordable as taking the family out for dinner. I would've never thought having a personal assistant would be that accessible to the everyday busy mom, like me. Check her out, she is amazing[177].

If I search for certain questions on voice and my voice assistant cannot answer it, then there may be an opportunity to capitalize on Google's desire to answer the question with the RIGHT answer.

I would recommend starting with Google. This interaction is called Implicit Invocation. As Google is scrambling to get more questions answered, your brand could potentially accelerate visibility to your site and your business while Google is in hyper growth mode on voice. Just something else to ponder.

You would also want to do a deeper SEO data dive to find related terms and questions, search engine rankings, and other variables to find the best potential phrases combined with the conversational data that you may have found.

The equivalent on Alexa is called CanFulfillIntent and is powerful, especially if you sell products on Amazon.

As Google and Alexa try desperately to outperform the other one, use this as an opportunity to capitalize and potentially accelerate your reach and visibility on voice.

VOICE TAKEAWAYS

There are always going to be fads and trends. Natural Language Processing (aka Voice) is already the next great wave. Voice is mass.

Much like emerging technology, it's a new frontier. That means it may require the same amount of focus, time, or effort of any other channel that your brand utilizes.

If you don't have a vast and validated deep understanding of your consumer, you had better get started – and now -- because the brands that really get their consumers will win on voice search and with voice assistants.

The good news is if you have a customer, you can validate your assumptions.

Voice offers the lowest barrier to entry of any other channel right now, with millions of opportunities that your brand can fulfill. Waiting to see what can happen with voice is no longer an option.

Following are a few ways to get started today:

- Find someone who LOVES copyrighting, dialogue, and conversations.
- Find or hire an amazing creative person.
- Find or hire a data nerd.
- Curiosity is a non-negotiable trait for this team.
- Gather those people and talk about voice.
- Give the team the time they need to ideate and think creatively.

- Ideate about how to leverage voice as a catalyst into the heart and the homes of your consumers.
- Embrace experimentation with the condition of constant optimization, and improvement.

Those who start **voice now** have the potential to **own, lead, and shape your category**.

The beauty of voice is everyone wins. The consumer has a voice assistant that gives her multiple experiences that make her life more fulfilling, saving her time, and saving her money. The brand wins because you are learning from consumers directly what conversations they want to have with your brand and which conversational touchpoints move the shopper closer to the cart, store, or business.

The foundation of voice combines machine processing to learn how to improve at a much faster pace than the human brain can, giving you an incredibly powerful advantage. As we evolve to the next level of consumer shopping experiences, voice will be one of the ways to differentiate your brand and become integrated into the daily lives and routines of your shopper.

Key Takeaways:

- Don't wait on voice. It's here and you need to be on it.
- Start with a narrow and focus on doing that one thing well.
- Design for future behaviors, don't stick to the same thing that everyone else is doing today.
- Validate as much as you can before you build your voice customer experience.
- Don't push commerce too quickly. You risk your damaging your trust and credibility.
- Identify what voice can make better in your current customer experience today.
- Look for opportunities to capture and mine conversational data.
- Create something transformative.

SECTION 3:
INNOVATION

IMAGINE A WORLD

I am a huge fan of Samsung. I am a die-hard, loyal Samsung customer. We have a lot of Samsung products in our home and I am always super excited when a new line is released.

Samsung has a refrigerator that I am going to own one day. It is simply incredible. The refrigerator has pressure sensors on the shelves. When I buy a gallon of milk and I put that milk on the shelf, the refrigerator detects how much weight is in that container. If I put 128 ounces of milk in the refrigerator, it's gone fast. The kids get cereal, and we make omelets, chocolate milk, milk and cookies, and we make hot chocolate (see a theme here?). Eventually the milk gets down to 30 ounces, then my refrigerator can let me know that it's time to buy milk. The refrigerator will automatically add milk to on my shopping list.

Did I mention that there are also four cameras within the refrigerator? You might think cameras sound creepy in a refrigerator. If I buy a pack of chicken breast with a sell-by date of the 13th, this amazing refrigerator can scan that date from the label and remind me -- on my refrigerator, on my phone, and my Google Home monitor -- that the chicken breast is about to expire if I don't use it before the 12th.

Likewise, if I buy organic pasture-raised salted butter and place it in my Samsung Smart refrigerator, when it sees that my butter is down to one stick, it will send me a message saying that there is a BOGO (buy one, get one) coupon on the brand it knows I prefer. Whenever there is a BOGO on anything that I buy, I will buy several of them because I feel like healthy food is never on sale! My fancy refrigerator can add the brand of butter I buy my shopping list, send me a notification to let me know that the butter is BOGO until Thursday. On Wednesday, if it detects that butter is on my list and not in my fridge, it will gently remind me on my voice speaker that the BOGO ends tomorrow. My voice assistant can look at my schedule, where it determines that my only opening is 3 p.m. today, so she asks me if I want my groceries ordered and delivered at 3 p.m.

How creepy are those cameras now?

This is not the future, this is now. How can you take experiences that you have with your customers to a new level?

You may think that the Samsung refrigerator is cool or just creepy, but psychologically, as a consumer I would pay for refrigerator to shop for me. Why?

- It's convenient.
- It saves me time.
- It's saves me money.
- It reduces the "things" I have to do in my life.
- It reduces my stress and eliminates my "Mommy Shame" of having no milk on a crazy morning when we just want to prepare a balanced breakfast.

My Samsung refrigerator isn't just a really big and expensive cool gadget. It gives me time to do the things that I want to do with my family. If my job was to sell the Samsung refrigerator, I wouldn't sell it based on features and the cool things that it can do. I would sell it to busy parents saying this refrigerator will allow you to be present and watch your kids grow up. That is what innovation does for brand.

Internet of Things (IoT) is a technology that many retailers could use with a thoughtful innovation strategy.

Amazon Dash Buttons were introduced in 2015, allowing consumers to use internet-enabled buttons to reorder common products that need to be replenished often.

Imagine common household products like toilet paper, paper towels, or laundry detergent could simply appear whenever your household is low. For example, a family of four might need laundry detergent every four weeks while a single man could go at least 10 weeks. If the retailers have access to consumer buying behaviors, preferences, and frequencies, there are so many possibilities

WHY INNOVATION FAILS

> *"We try to rationalize why innovations from other sectors don't apply to us, rather than focusing on why they do."*
>
> – George Blankenship

In this crazy, fast-paced world, we often have to focus on too many things at once, which prevents us from being fully committed to any of them. As leaders, we are often expected to bring creative solutions to problems but are not given the time to sit and think about the best way to solve the problem. You can't be a jack of all trades and master of none. In most companies, you are running from meeting to meeting without time to work, much less think. According to MIT, the average executive spends *23 hours a week in meetings*[190]. We need more time than in the shower every morning or on our run to just think about solutions.

In a Charlie Rose interview with Bill Gates and Warren Buffet, Bill Gates said the most valuable lesson he learned from Warren Buffet was about time[191]. Gates goes on to talk about how his work life was scheduled to the minute. He felt like as the CEO people needed him, and it was his duty and responsibility to see everyone that needed to see him. Warren Buffet pulls out his small, handwritten pocket calendar and shows week after week of wide-

---

[190] *Say OK Google - Talk to Discovered Book – MIT Research Study*

[191] *Say OK Google - Talk to Discovered Book – Bill Gates*

open days of time. Buffet goes on to talk about how important time is, noting that it is the one thing that all the money in the world cannot buy more of. Gates has learned to be very protective of his time.

Now you may think, "I'm not Warren Buffett or Bill Gates, I have people I report to, other executives, shareholders, board members, or a demanding overly unrealistic boss." I get it. But I know there is something that can be done to change that time dynamically. This is not some "kumbaya" time to take every day to meditate to have a deeply spiritual journey. This is not the time that you want to randomly cyber stalk your competitor or get a mental break with mindlessly distracting cat videos.

Every leader and their team should have time to:

- Think
- Focus
- Ideate
- Create
- Innovate

Regardless of whether or not you are fans of Bill Gates or Warren Buffet, you may respect what they have accomplished. Bill Gates doesn't attribute the success of Microsoft as his legacy, rather he believes his legacy is eliminating diseases, giving underprivileged kids access to technology, providing clean water, and hundreds of other initiatives that The Gates Foundation has funded. Without Microsoft, they couldn't have made the world a better place. Microsoft was the catalyst to allow real change to happen on a global scale. I am sure there are warm fuzzy stories about Microsoft, but who really cares about the business impact Word has had on the world of executive assistants or PowerPoint stories by sales veterans? Many of us are here to make the world better. How on earth are you expected to do that if the only time you have to think is on your commute to and from work?

Yes, we are getting older. Yes, no one has more time in their day. Yes, we are all busy. These aren't new things that I am talking about. Sadly, these are all given in our lives today. To say it more bluntly, if you are not given the time you and your team need to ideate, think, or focus, you may not be able to innovate or change at all. You may have heard the saying "If you aren't growing, you're dying." Growth is a part of innovation. And growth and learning are at the core of innovation.

Now that we have beat time to death, how does this affect our success or failure? Tremendously. If we don't have time to think, we are in a constant state of reacting and responding as quickly as possible. That shows up as the same marketing that everyone else is doing. More of the same.

What can you shift today to create just 20 minutes of free time per day? What can you stop doing or delegate? Look for something that you know is not the best use of your time. We all have many things that fit into this category. If your day is just jam packed, channel our friends Warren and Gates, and commit to waking up earlier or ending your day later.

Amazon is this terrible beast in the eyes of many brands and retailers. We look at Amazon as this universe-sized monster that is here only to destroy our brands and wipe out years of history.

However, I have mad respect for Jeff Bezos in some aspects and not so much in others. In November 2018, during the Amazon shareholder meeting Jeff Bezos said this to his employees:

"One day, Amazon will fail but our job is to delay it as long as possible."

– Jeff Bezos

Bezos goes on to explain that Amazon will be disrupted by another company and may follow the traditional retailer's path to doom... bankruptcy. He has the foresight to build a business to delay the demise as long as he can. Come on, who can't respect that? If you have the foresight as a leader to think that way in the same year your business blows past the $200B mark? I certainly can.

Take Sears for example. Sears was an innovator many times over...

- Sears was the first to bring catalogs and shopping into homes in 1902[192].
- Sears added anchor stores to malls during WWI to help small suburban towns survive hard economic times.
- Sears was the first major retailer to offer consumer credit with the store, allowing people to finance the refrigerator or stove that just went kaput in their homes.
- By the 1990s, one of seven Americans worked or had worked for Sears[193].
- Sears created an omnichannel effect before omnichannel became the most used buzzword in the marketing realm for the last decade.
- Sears wasn't the first of just one thing; they were the first of many.

---

[192] *Say OK Google - Talk to Discovered Book – How Sears Changed America*

[193] *Say OK Google - Talk to Discovered Book – Rise & Fall of Sears*

Sears changed people's lives, shifted how consumers bought, and paved the way for thousands of retailers for decades to come.

Sears didn't stop innovating when digital and eCommerce started to take over; instead, they:

- Created millions of online shopping channels.
- Launched free shipping in 2010, just like Amazon Prime, which started in 2006.
- Offered curbside delivery and pickup of orders well before Walmart and Target.
- Made significant investments into mobile website responsiveness well before Google forewarned eCommerce sites to start to think about getting ready for mobile.

Sears started to waver when a perfect storm was brewing of physical competition, the birth of the digital revolution, and an economic downturn with over-leveraged debt. The big box retailers like Walmart and Home Depot were in the same cities as their staple Sears retail stores.

Since the 1800s, Sears was recognized as the retailer that cared about making it convenient for the consumer. They were still innovating but quickly losing their perceived value and relationships with their consumer base. Other companies were also focusing on making consumers' lives easier with online and offline solutions, too. In addition, the in-store shopping experience was not exactly engaging. When was the last time that you chose to go to

Sears first over another retail option? Consumers are so heavily engaged with different online experiences and retail experiences from other retailers that walking into a Sears store today feels like you are walking into a Sears store from the 1990s.

Innovation is a mindset. A constant state of being curious and not accepting that how it's being done today is the only way or even the best way. Innovation is not just the practice of doing something new, but fostering a culture of growth and creativity with dedicated time to think and focus. Innovation is something that is possible with any person, any team, and in any company. Even if it seems like an impossible task right now, it doesn't have to be.

A new category of innovation

Amazon is a company that is often referred to as "innovative." You don't have to compare Amazon's years of honing in on their innovative practices and culture to where you are right now. It's like comparing the poor black girl from Alabama at 6 to Oprah when she made her first billion. It's not a fair comparison at all.

Just to give you an understanding of how important Amazon has made innovation, here is a high-level overview of the process they follow with new ideas or innovative ideas[194].

- All innovation starts with a six-page memo. Yes, an actual old-school memorandum. This is a process that forces employees to take the time they need to think through your ideas fully and completely.
- Amazon's culture is deeply obsessed with putting the customer first. It requires the idea to be looked through the lens of the customer's eyes: examining the customer's feelings, objections, confusion, and

---

194 *Say OK Google - Talk to Discovered Book – Amazon Innovation*

even the friction within the experience of the idea.

- In addition to creating a better experience for the customers through this process, Amazon also considers the decision makers and objections they may have.

"You often need to go slow to move fast."

Amazon's innovation creation process forces you to take things slower, not faster. The creative process doesn't start with a PowerPoint deck or a kickoff meeting. It starts by writing. As journalist Fareed Zakaria once put it, "Thinking and writing are inextricably intertwined. When I begin to write, I realize that my 'thoughts' are usually a jumble of half-baked, incoherent impulses strung together with gaping logical holes between them."

The process to innovate is one that could take a week for an idea to make it through multiple teams to review and provide feedback to the idea owner. Once everyone has given feedback, the idea is meeting-worthy.

Meetings start with 30-60 minutes of reading the finished innovative idea memo. Then, they gather first-gut responses, leaving management's feedback for last. Just to put things in terms of time to market, Amazon's Prime Now, their one-hour delivery service, took 111 days from ideation to product launch of one-hour delivery into one zip code in Manhattan.

Companies enter the marketplace every day.

Consider Local Motors, which builds a completely customized car in one afternoon and has pivoted to providing multi-person autonomous transportation akin to mini buses that look like a Fiat smart car without a driver like an airport train[195].

---

[195] *Say OK Google - Talk to Discovered Book – Local Motors*

Consider Quirky, which can take your idea and create a fully functional prototype ready to go to market in less than 30 days[196].

Companies can no longer take their sweet time to react and respond. By reacting to market changes, economic factors, consumer changes, and distractions with more of the same, you could be risking everything.

There is no magic way to innovate. Every company has a mission, purpose, culture, and drive which flows over into how they innovate.

For example:

- Apple has a fanatical focus on design and lifestyle that drives new ideas and products.
- IBM's commitment to technology has allowed them to be an industry giant for decades.
- Google combines many innovative strategies into a seamless experience.

If you are open to learning how to use technology to innovate, you can both learn a lot and have a ton of fun along the way.

If you are looking for a better way to increase sales and are open to trying something new, then this is for you!

---

[196] *Say OK Google - Talk to Discovered Book – Quirky*

"Awareness is like the sun.
When it shines on things, they are transformed."

– Thich Nhat Hanh

With my last 20 years spent on leveraging the latest technology to gain a marketing and sales advantage, I have never been more excited than this moment we are in right now. We are at the cusp of connecting technologies that will improve the lives of millions of people's customer experiences.

The barrier to innovate has never been lower the speed of innovation has never been faster. You have a small window of opportunity to leverage these technologies before they are so widely adopted that you lose your vantage point. With the convergence of 5G networks, multiple virtual and augmented realities, deep learning and machined algorithms, the options are nearly limitless. The direction of how consumers behave on their unique buying journeys will continue to evolve and the choice is yours whether you want your brand to be found on those buying journeys or not.

It is not too late to not only win the game but change the rules.

"Shall we play a game?"

War Games[197]

---

[197] *Say OK Google - Talk to Discovered Book – Shall we play a game?*

INNOVATING CUSTOMER EXPERIENCES

"Innovation distinguishes between a leader and a follower."

– Steve Jobs

There are so many studies done on Millennials and how they shop. It is a hot topic for brands to understand how to reach, engage, and influence this demographic.

One study found that 48% Millennials value the experience they have with the brand more than the product itself. Which is the opposite of Baby Boomers, who value the product while only 22% value the experience more[200]. Millennials believe their greatest predictor of loyalty is the experience with the brand.

Shopping online is often referred to as a passive experience where we have a highly visual experience of imagery and an auditory experience with sounds, so the focus is on those two senses. It is scientifically proven that cognitive recall of physical store experience is far greater than that of online experiences. In the store, you can hit all of the senses beyond just sight and sound, smell, and touch and, ultimately, how the experience makes people feel.

---

[200] *Say OK Google - Talk to Discovered Book – Millennials Value Experience*

Physical experiences are a more powerful and meaningful than any other form of media. Don't take my word for it, it's science!

If your brand can offer unique experiences leveraging technology and a physical aspect do so wherever it creates a valuable experience, you will be ahead of your competition. There are so many options for brands today to have a physical location even if it's just in a short period of time.

eCommerce only brands are breaking into physical spaces with pop-ups. Birchbox, the subscription brand company, has started opening retail locations.

For example, Storefront, helps brands find temporary space rental from a few hours to a few months, depending on the brand's needs.

Physical + Digital Experiences = Phygital

Sephora has taken what most retailers perceived as a challenge and incorporated it into the shopping experience in the physical store. Brands and retailers shudder knowing that the consumer is seeing hundreds of options on their phones as opposed to just focusing on what is on the shelf right in front of them. Instead of shying away from digital phone usage when in the store, Sephora decided to embrace it.

Their innovation team understood that the mobile shopping experience was much different than the in-store shopping experience. Online, there are hundreds of SKUs for a single product category, like lipstick. When people get in the store, they wanted to compare only a few products and see reviews. But the experience to get down to just those select products within the store was no different than it was if someone was shopping online.

Sephora created an app that would recognize when customers were in the store based on smartphone GPS.

The app asks customers if they want to switch to in-store mode. The in-store shopping experience doesn't show all 3,000 lipsticks as it would online, instead, it shows three to five different lipsticks in stock now paired with the information that the shopper is already looking for in terms of reviews and comparisons. This adds value to the shopping experience for the shopper in-store. While in-store, the shopper preferences (data) are utilized to give the shopper a custom and personalized experience. We know that people are using their phones in the store, we see it every day. How can you make it easier to buy your brand?

Sephora has also tested other innovations like workstations. A Sephora assistant will teach you, inspire you, and even schedule a makeup consultation in the store on digital kiosks. These kiosks combine physical and digital in one experience, which is actually termed "phygital."[201]

When we set off on our innovation journey, we don't know which idea will be a slam dunk and which one will just be a slam. This is why creating a culture of experimentation and constant optimization is key. Because you may not get it 100% right the first time. If you do, please call me, we're hiring!

In-Store Experiences

Retailers are leveraging experiential and in-store activations by creating fresh interactive and fun shopper experiences. This is sometimes called "retail-tainment" by some mega-retailers. These in store events can be interactive and tech-forward with apps using augmented reality or virtual reality to engage with people, not only in

[201] *Say OK Google - Talk to Discovered Book – Sephora*

person but beyond to social media, email, eCommerce, vCommerce, all the way through to checkout.

This is a really exciting time in retail with so many emerging technologies that can impact experiences both online and in-store. Many of these technologies will help retailers create a deeper connection with the consumer to help drive in-store sales.

As search continues to evolve well beyond the standard Google search terms of "How do I" or "Where can I find," our brands need to be prepared for turning our search content into conversations.

Leveraging Schema Markup will allow retailers to be found through organic search not only during the initial research but when the consumer is using search again within the store. Many stores, like Walmart are using beacons to monitor where you are in the store. If you are in their Walmart app and you search for an item, the app will tell you what aisle the item is in. Then you will see yourself on the store floorplan and location pins to where you should be going. This can help me find my items faster and giving me a better, and faster shopping experience. Walmart's app is pretty slick. It is worth taking a look at. Check out the voice capability built in to their app too!

As mentioned earlier, the book "Reengineering Retail" by Doug Stephens is a must, must, must read for any future-focused brand or retailer[24]. He gives some super cool examples of how people are taking the in-store experience, which is typically a very dull and boring experience, and making it an interactive engaging experience with their consumers. Doug believes that the store is the media channel and the experience sells more than any advertising campaign every could.

In New York City, Sonos sells speakers systems for home. The Sonos store includes a fully immersed surround-sound experience for your daily life[202]. You enter home pods, which look like cozy living rooms. Each pod has Sonos speakers installed exactly as you would in your own home. You can sit in your living room pod to listen to perfectly acoustically tuned music. Each pod is soundproofed and super comfy so you can choose your favorite music, sit back, and relax quite literally.

Sonos understood that the world doesn't need another electronic store where you can press buttons and listen to five sound systems that all sound the same. I don't know about you but I spend more time trying to recognize the difference between the five blue buttons, rather than listening to the quality of the sound. I'm probably just weird like that. What consumers really wanted was a beautiful space where they can gather and celebrate the unique central joy of listening to music. Sonos gives you a listening experience that is fun and shareworthy; you can bring your friends, since they can fit in the listening living room pod, too.

Another store that gets the in-store experience right is Globetrotters, which has retail spaces like amusement parks for outdoors-loving people[203]. There are high-altitude chambers were customers can prepare themselves for a major ascend. You can check out their 220,000-liter scuba diving tank. Or maybe you'd rather dive, paddle, and sail in the store's canoeing and kayaking pool so you can try out the equipment before you buy it. There's a glass climbing tunnel where enthusiasts and novices can try out gear. They have an arctic chamber where you can test cold-weather equipment and clothing. They even have a storm chamber where you can test waterproof clothing in what feels like a tsunami weather conditions.

---

[202] *Say OK Google - Talk to Discovered Book – Sonos*

[203] *Say OK Google - Talk to Discovered Book – Globetrotters*

Each area of the store provides the opportunity to actually experience the products. Even the shoe department has trail runs that feel just like hiking surfaces outside so you can actually feel the traction and comfort of the shoes.

The bathroom toilets are designed to simulate the tiny bathrooms found on ships. They even have feature screens in the bathroom that show exotic scenery passing by, like you're really on a ship!

If that wasn't enough, their stores also have immunization clinics for malaria, yellow fever, and other diseases. They offer on-site travel agents who can help you book your next adventure. You can even schedule to stay overnight in the store to test your camp and tent gear.

Globetrotters has turned the outdoor gear-shopping experience into a destination – a destination that has reviews on TripAdvisor. Not only is this an incredible experience for their customers, it has earned them countless sources of earned media. Globetrotters core value is the authentic story with a love and deep passion for adventure and the outdoors.

Another amazing example of amazing in-store experience exists in Pirch, a home improvement store. At Pirch you get to try your home appliances, fixtures, etc *before* you buy[204].

Looking for a new shower head? Bring your bathing suit to test their models to see which one tickles your fancy, quite literally. Working on a kitchen remodel? By all means, come in and cook dinner. You can cook a meal alongside a professional chef, across several different cooktops and ovens and experience what it would feel like to cook on the Viking versus the Five Star.

Pirch is beautifully decorated and inspiring. The walls are covered with quotes like "Tomorrow is promised to no

---

[204] *Say OK Google - Talk to Discovered Book – Pirch*

one" or "Make time for family. In the end, they are everything." Their philosophy is to make customers feel like their time in the store is the best part of the day, whether they buy something or not.

If these examples seem massive or overwhelming, remember that you don't have to build out a full retail space to create a memorable experience in store. You can make minor investments in innovation and dedicate a portion of the square footage of the store to test.

Lowe's has piloted robots to guide people directly to the aisle of product they want[205]. Instead of asking an associate where you can find packing bubble wrap, ask the friendly little robot. The robot will lead you to the exact location and see if it can take you to the next item on the list. It may even prompt you to see if you need packing tape, which you could have totally forgotten about. I can't tell you how many times I have been in the middle of a project and realized I was out of one thing. I stop working on the project to go get that one thing, only to realize a couple of hours later that I am missing something else. I would totally listen to the robot, that knows better than I do, what complementary supplies may be useful to buy right now while at the store.

Lowe's also created a virtual reality home improvement pod where you can work with a design specialist to create a virtual space similar to the one you are shopping for[206]. Using virtual reality headsets, you can choose and see the exact fixtures, finishes, and decor you have chosen to get an idea of what it would really look like. The Lowe's specialist will ask questions about your selection and change the design in real time as you look around the room. Maybe you thought copper would match that white

---

205 *Say OK Google - Talk to Discovered Book – LoweBot*

206 *Say OK Google - Talk to Discovered Book – Lowes HoloLens*

sink perfectly but you're hesitating? The Lowe's associate recommends a brushed steel. And you love it! Nothing is worse than paying a lot of money for something you don't like! You can also check out the full case study done by Microsoft[207].

For retailers, shifting focus to price per square foot is not going to be an easy task. This has been the key driver for retailers for decades. Another measure of success is the **customer experience index**. This value has generated more direct financial impact on brands that excel at customer experience than price per square foot.

According to Forrester, a stock portfolio of leading companies and their customer experience index had a cumulative performance gain of 43% over six years compared to the average 14.5% for this S&P 500. When the customer experience index lacks, brands historically see a drop of 33.9%[208].

The customer experience, if done well, **will** have a direct impact on the bottom line.

Research has shown companies that outperform with customer experience generate a **dramatic increase in revenues**.

[207] *Say OK Google - Talk to Discovered Book - HoloLens Case Study*

[208] *Say OK Google - Talk to Discovered Book - Customer Experience Index*

Retailers that are future-focused on the experience with their consumers may be the last one standing as shopping changes, home grocery delivery becomes commonplace, and people abandon trips to the store.

If you're a retailer, where can you use portions of the floor as media? Most retailers get more foot traffic in a year to their store than they do their website. You don't have to be elaborate with listening living room pods or walking trails but determine where you can you start to shift your store into an experience?

If you are struggling for ideas on how to make this happen, see if you have a Lush Cosmetics store near you. It is not really *just* cosmetics, it's more of a body lotion, shampoo store, including products for men. Just look for one near you and visit. That is an in-store experience.

Understanding Consumer Preferences

The Globetrotter retail store understood their customers so well that they offered complementary services to make their lives easier. Globetrotter sold outdoorspeople equipment but offered immunizations and travel agent services, elevating the experience with their brand.

REI builds the in-store experience based on validated customer data and touchpoints[38]. They are always curious, always testing, and always optimizing.

By leveraging machine learning through voice, you may gain greater insight to help your customers. too. In my household, we do not eat certain foods that are genetically modified, contain high-fructose corn syrup, or have traces of pesticides (I hope). I personally drive further to Earth Fare because the store's values match my family's health values. But a retailer could and should know my preferences and give me the options that I would be more likely to buy.

If a retailer knows that people are vegan or gluten free, then their food options will be much different than someone who is on a high-protein meat diet. There are more options than most of us care to think about. That is where artificial intelligence, machine learning, and deep learning can help.

Leveraging inventory data and consumer buying preferences with deep learning can help busy consumers differentiate one retailer from the rest.

There is always room for improvement. There is always a way to reduce friction. Start to think of ways that your brand can begin to bring innovation to your consumer experiences. If you are drawing a blank, no worries, that is why we hire people way smarter than us. Bring it to your team. Create a challenge. Create a new volunteer innovation team. Just start.

BRAND INNOVATION

Remember when TiVo first came out? This great little box allowed you to record a show from your television. It was revolutionary. Even better, the remote had a 30-second skip button, which was awesome news for consumers who loved to skip commercials. But it was terrifying for advertisers because we just gave consumers the power to ignore our ads.

TiVo disrupted the TV watching experience by giving TV fans a way to watch their favorite TV show at a later date in time. It was incredible. As a result, TiVo also allowed consumers to bypass commercials altogether Also, incredible.

This helped advertisers begin to think of new and creative ways that they could reach consumers, which they had otherwise relied on through commercials. And even though commercials are hard to measure and quantify the results, they are still a huge chunk of many brand's marketing budgets. Brand awareness is important and historically has been a challenge to measure.

Today, we seem to have more and more data yet we don't feel empowered with the insight that we need to make better decisions. As we enter the world of smart experiences, where everything is connected and many things can be measured, we will find volumes of mind-blowing data. Not all data is meaningful. It is essential that your brand has visibility to the data that delivers insight and helps you make better, more informed decisions to drive sales. The rest of the data, I really could care less about.

It's not easy being a brand that has to compete for shelf space in the store, often against a retailer's private labels and emerging brands that seem to pop up every single day. If you are competing online, e-commerce can be equally challenging with the high cost to advertise or losing margin on channels like Amazon or Walmart.com. It leaves very little room for profit.

Brands will have to continue to think of creative ways to innovate to survive and thrive in a rapidly changing, consumer-driven, and fiercely competitive environment.

This new paradigm of direct to consumer has created an opportunity for consumers to shape the direction of products that they most desire. There are companies that have been created to help brands gather rapid research and understanding about the consumer experience necessary to make a product or plan successful.

Rachel Shechtman created the company Story, a store located in Manhattan's Lower West Side. Story is a physical location that gives the point of view of the magazine but it changes like a gallery while it sells things like the store. Her background in media and retail gave her the point of view to turn square footage into an in-person media channel. People might spend 30 seconds flipping through a magazine, which can only partially tell the story of the brand. The Story team and store gets paid to tell the stories for the brands. And it's not a cheap story. Her minimum was $600,000 to create a story with one of her editors and for your product to be placed in her gallery for a few weeks of time. Want the coveted holiday season time? That will be $1 million please. You may think that that price tag is high, but is much less than what you pay for a commercial to tell the story in 30 seconds, not knowing if it is having an impact on sales or not.

Rachel was creating experiences before experiential retail was a thing. She started with the story of the brand being displayed in the store and using the store as the media channel. She focuses on the community aspect of retail that is often overlooked and underrated.

Macy's acquired Story in April 2018 and you can read about what she and Macy's are up to with their new "community retail" play[209].

We are reaching a similar paradigm with conversational experiences. Story was a team or writers and editors, not marketers. They created stories to connect with shoppers. Voice may require new skills and talent of creative writing or persuasive copyrighters to master the art of conversation. Be open as you enter this new realm of possibility that you may need to introduce new skills or people to your team.

---

[209] *Say OK Google - Talk to Discovered Book – Retail as the media*

INNOVATION TAKEAWAYS

Everyone will be disrupted, even Jeff Bezos is expecting the disruption of Amazon in the future. The question is: Will your brand embrace innovation and be the disruptor or will someone else comes along who will move faster than you? And will they move so quickly that you won't be able to catch up, or as Doug Stephens says, "Can you put yourself out of business before they do?"

As technology advances, we will be able to do so much more with our brands, interactivity, and our shoppers.

Companies that are at the forefront of innovation by integrating the internet beyond smartphones, voice, and search will succeed.

This technology already exists and is being used daily by millions of consumers, the challenge is figuring out what your brand's innovative experience could be.

If you can dream it, it most likely can be built it, if hasn't been built already.

Key Takeaways:

- Innovation is not a word on a wall, it is a culture and mindset.
- Innovation has to be supported from the top.
- Innovation requires uncommon ways of thinking.
- Innovation does not have a hard ROI, don't build a business case around ROI.
- Innovation isn't for every brand and that's ok.
- Don't strive to out innovate your competition, strive to out innovate yourself.

CONCLUSION

Being innovative may be seen as a risk. You may not have years of proof. There may not be dozens of experts. But I truly believe that those who embrace the power of Schema and Voice will not only have a first-mover advantage in the near term but will have a future-proof competitive edge for the long term.

We do the best we can with the information that we have. In many cases, yes, it's an assumption. But if we can enrich our experiences with our consumers with better insight based off of real conversations, then we can continue to improve those experiences with customers and shoppers.

Much like this lean startup methodology, it is important to understand that not everything is going to return massive results or is going to take off like we think it is. But if we continue to stay curious and continue to validate assumptions, then we can deliver the experiences that our consumers are yearning to have with our brands.

The key is being open to doing something differently. Do not allow past experience and bias to prevent an idea that would come to life which could transform relationships with shoppers. There is a price to pay to be first. There is a risk to bear when you go against the norm. But to continue to follow the pack and do the same thing better than your competitor will only get you so far.

This might not be an easy sell in your organization. If you run a risk-averse machine, then you may have no other choice but to sit back and wait. I beg to differ. If the barrier of entry into a brand-new channel, that it is estimated to grow to $80 billion by 2023, then can you afford to not enter that channel now?

Owning the Conversation

In an effort to grow and scale our brands, many of us have distribution channels that are necessary but don't return much profit. In some cases, these retailers and channels don't make it easy to control or influence our brand's purpose and value. It gets lost on the shelf and in the world created and controlled by our retail partners.

There is value in owning your brand's voice.

You can own that brand voice with four things:

1. Content that fulfills intent;
2. Schema that gives meaning to answer engines;
3. Voice that starts an engaging conversation;
4. Community that supports and loves your products.

Content should be owned and controlled by your brand. It is necessary for Schema to be successful. Every brand has content that they own and control. It does not have to be eCommerce; it just has to be content that you own and control.

Schema is applied to content with the context and semantics to help answer engines understand:

- Your brand's voice
- Your brand's purpose
- What makes your brand unique
- Your brand's usefulness or utility
- Your reviews and ratings, customer feedback, and social proof
- Your brand's channels (the ones you want to highlight and drive sales to)
- Your brand's connections (between social, products,

videos, recipes, reviews, events, and so on)

Voice experiences are a fit for every brand but the strategy should be one that delivers a delightful experience and is based on validated data. Voice is mass now. Brands that embrace voice with the right strategy are creating a future-proof position to shape and lead their category.

Create a Religion

Communities are worth their weight in gold. Peloton has built an incredible community. A friend told me she has three Pelotons in her house: two bikes and one treadmill. That is $15,000 worth of consumer community love right there.

She started riding first, then her husband wanted to ride, so she bought a second bike and a treadmill. She rode with her community of people regularly and they have developed a larger community. Her tribe of fellow riders threw her a virtual baby shower. They all met at a specified time to ride, and when the ride was over her doorbell rang and she opened the door to a porch filled with baby shower gifts. That was a community-created and -organized event. A community is a powerful thing. When you treat your consumers well, they will be your disciples and they will advocate for your brand without ever being asked to do so.

Start with a community but strive for a religion. People relentlessly defend their religion. You want a cult-like community that is ride or die for your brand, metaphorically speaking.

Future-Proofing Your Brand

Forward-thinking brands are always trying to outthink their competition. One way is to future-proof your brand Wayne Gretzky style.

> *"Skate to where the puck is going, not where it has been."*
>
> – Wavne Gretzkv

Stop trying to beat your competition by doing what they do but better. Create a real future-proof strategy that will ensure that you not only lead but your competition can't even respond because their heads are spinning so fast.

If your brand executes a Schema and voice strategy while strengthening your direct-to-consumer channel, you are creating a future-proof advantage that your competition can't displace with all the ad money in the world.

Start somewhere today

Whether you have an entire team with millions of dollars in marketing spend or you are an emerging challenger brand with a small team of two, voice is for you.

Here are some easy ways to get started today:

- You can start with a small lean team.
- Give them a small task to ideate how you can leverage voice to reach and engage and connect with

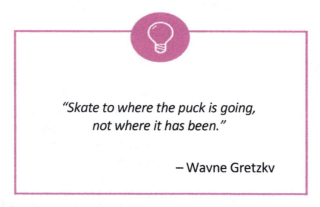

your consumers.

- Don't influence.
- Support but don't lead.
- Consider all the options and ideas. Bad ideas make good ideas stronger.
- Take the Amazon approach and socialize ideas to the leadership team.
- Always view the idea through the lens of the customer.
- Poke holes in the plan. Pros and cons, best case, worst case, and determine collectively if this is an idea worth validating with your shoppers.
- If you validate the idea with your consumer base, try to engage with as many ideal consumers as possible. By ideal, I mean consumers with the highest lifetime value to your brand.
- Talk to a statistically viable number of people based on your market size and perform an analysis to determine whether or not it's a go or no-go.

Sales will always be the key measure of success in business but if you have the philosophy that your customers matter, your service to them matters, then voice is a natural play for your brand.

If you have retail space, consider measuring customer experience index as another potential metric of success.

Customer Experiences

We care about our customers. Our products solve problems. Add value and make the lives of our shoppers easier. We believe in what we do. And there is nothing more frustrating than spending precious time, resources, and money trying to reach the people who are looking for us but they're not finding us.

Right now, you can combine the insight and knowledge that you know is true about your consumers and shift the thinking from keywords to intent and speakable so you can start to be found as the answer on voice.

Imagine all of the incredible stories, resources, and content that you have to share with the millions of people trying to find your brand. **You don't have to start big, you just have to start.**

Throughout this book, I've shared resources that have helped me understand this new frontier. But I also understand that this can be incredibly overwhelming and complex to explain and comprehend.

If your brand would like our help or you want to reach us, visit Discoveredbook.com/ Start.

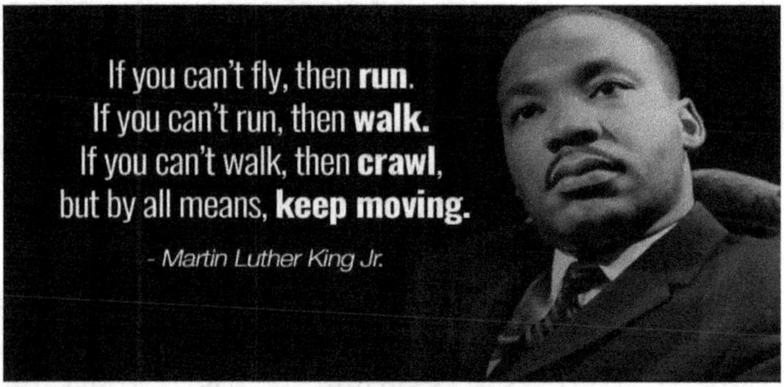

If you can't fly, then run.
If you can't run, then walk.
If you can't walk, then crawl,
but by all means, keep moving.
- Martin Luther King Jr.

SOURCES

3 Easy ways to find the sources in this book:

Super Easy: Google Assistant – Just say "*Talk to Discovered Book*". Then say the phrase next to the 🎙. *ie* 🎙 *Phrase*

Kinda Easy: Visit https://DiscoveredBook.com/Book - Click on the Chapter Name, find the Footnote Number and click. That will direct you to the correct source link.

Old School: If you are reading the print copy of the book, type the source with the super long links below.

Introduction

1. 🎙 *Martech Image* –Over 7,000 Marketing Solutions https://chiefmartec.com/2019/04/marketing-technology-landscape-supergraphic-2019/

2. 🎙 *Martech Companies* – Google sheet to download of the current Martech Companies https://docs.google.com/forms/d/e/1FAIpQLSeww-FTtVQRby9DjNp7DVxYHmK6FCjhul7dPJZjgIGJiVU_wA/viewform

3. 🎙 *Deloitte Search* – 84% of people start the customer journey with search, Deloitte Digital Divide - https://www2.deloitte.com/insights/us/en/industry/retail-distribution/digital-divide-changing-consumer-behavior.html (US Edition) https://www2.deloitte.com/global/en/pages/consumer-business/articles/gx-global-digital-divide-

retail.html (Global Edition)

4. *Forrester Search* – 90% search along the buying journey, A Forrester Consulting, Thought Leadership Paper https://www.catalystdigital.com/wp-content/uploads/WhySearchPlusSocialEqualsSuccess-Catalyst.pdf
5. *Voicebot.ai SEO Report* - Voice Assistant SEO Report For Brands, Voicebot.ai https://Voicebot.ai/voice-assistant-seo-report-for-brands/

Preface

6. *Topher Morrison* - Amazing Strategist and solves big problems http://www.tophermorrison.com/
7. *KPI* - Key Person of Influence Book by Daniel Priestley with Foreword by Topher Morrison, https://amzn.to/2W9QzUP
8. *$80 Billion* - Estimated Annual Sales by 2023, 3.25B on Voice, 8B on Voice by 2023, Juniper, *Digital Voice Assistants in Use to Triple,* https://www.juniperresearch.com/press/press-releases/digital-voice-assistants-in-use-to-triple
9. *1 Billion Google Assistants* - Voicebot.ai, Google Assistant to be Available on 1 Billion Devices This Month – 10x More Than Alexa, https://Voicebot.ai/2019/01/07/google-assistant-to-be-available-on-1-billion-devices-this-month-10x-more-than-alexa/
10. *$17 Million Lost* – Lost Revenue in First Half of 2019 due to Lack of Search Visibility, Voicebot.ai, New Analysis Says NYT Best Sellers Will Lose $17 Million in 2019 Because of Voice Search Issues, https://Voicebot.ai/2019/03/11/new-analysis-says-nyt-best-sellers-will-lose-17-million-in-2019-because-

of-voice-search-issues-google-assistant-and-cortana-perform-best/

11. 🎙 *Voice Responses* - Voicebot.ai SEO Report, Voice Assistant SEO Report For Brands, Voicebot.ai https://Voicebot.ai/voice-assistant-seo-report-for-brands/
12. 🎙 *Third Party Responses* - Voicebot.ai SEO Report, Voice Assistant SEO Report For Brands, Voicebot.ai https://Voicebot.ai/voice-assistant-seo-report-for-brands/
13. 🎙 *Shopping Responses* - Voicebot.ai SEO Report, Voice Assistant SEO Report For Brands, Voicebot.ai https://Voicebot.ai/voice-assistant-seo-report-for-brands/
14. 🎙 *Business Investments in Voice* - Voicebot.ai, *Adobe Says 91% of Business Decision Makers Investing in Voice Today and Voice Commerce is the Top Objective of 45%*, https://Voicebot.ai/2019/05/14/adobe-says-91-of-business-decision-makers-investing-in-voice-today-and-voice-commerce-is-the-top-objective-of-45/
15. 🎙 *Daily Voice Habits* - Voicebot.ai, *Voice Assistant Consumer Adoption Report 2018*, https://Voicebot.ai/voice-assistant-consumer-adoption-report-2018/
16. 🎙 *Purchased on Voice* - PwC, *Prepare for the Voice Revolution*, https://www.pwc.com/us/en/services/consulting/library/consumer-intelligence-series/voice-assistants.html
17. 🎙 *Direct to Consumers* - 40% of consumer brands sell direct to customers, PwC Global Insights, *It's time for a consumer-centered metric: introducing 'return on experience'*, https://www.pwc.com/us/en/advisory-

services/ publications/ consumer-intelligence-series/ pwc-consumer-intelligence-series-customer-experience.pdf

18. 🎙 *Return on Experience* - Almost 1/ 3 consumers buy online weekly or more frequently, PwC Global Insights, *It's time for a consumer-centered metric: introducing 'return on experience',* https:/ / www.pwc.com/ us/ en/ advisory-services/ publications/ consumer-intelligence-series/ pwc-consumer-intelligence-series-customer-experience.pdf
19. 🎙 *Nike's Direct Play* - Nike's shift to focus on Direct-to-consumer channel, Phalguni Soni, "*Prospects Look Upbeat for Nike's Direct-to-Consumer Channel Stores,*" Market Realist, https:/ / marketrealist.com/ 2015/ 09/ prospects-look-upbeat-for-nikes-direct-to-consumer-channel/
20. 🎙 *Amazon Mobile Ads* - Amazon to launches mobile ads posing a threat to Google and Facebook, Spencer Soper, *Amazon to Launch Mobile Ads, in a Threat to Google and Facebook,* https:/ / www.bloomberg.com/ news/ articles/ 2019-03-21/ amazon-said-to-launch-mobile-ads-in-threat-to-google-facebook

Bumpy Road of Innovation

21. 🎙 *Foster Kids Need Us* - Dismal Foster Kid Stats, we need to change this for our kid's sakes! National Foster Youth Institute, *51 Useful Aging Out of Foster Care Statistics | Social Race Media,* https:/ / www.nfyi.org/ 51-useful-aging-out-of-foster-care-statistics-social-race-media/

Innovation and Technology

22. *Number of websites* - Total number of websites today, Internet Live Stats, https://www.internetlivestats.com/total-number-of-websites/
23. *Number of searches* - 3.5 Billion Google searches per day, Google searches per day, Internet Live Stats,https://www.internetlivestats.com/google-search-statistics/
24. *Reengineering Retail* – Book by Doug Stephens, Reengineering Retail Book - https://amzn.to/2WJ2t8n

Imagine a World - Search

30. *Movies* - Visual Movie Booking without clicking - Thank you Schema Markup and AMC

Search Behavior

31. *Black Buying Power* - Nielsen Report: "*Black Girl Magic" And Brand Loyalty Is Propelling Total Black Buying Power Toward $1.5 Trillion By 2021*, https://www.nielsen.com/us/en/press-room/2017/nielsen-report-black-girl-magic-and-brand-loyalty-is-propelling-black-buying-power.html
32. *Black Girl Magic* - The Study on the Psychology behind Black Girl Magic and the influence online Nielsen Report: *African-American Women: Our Science*, Her Magic, https://www.nielsen.com/us/en/insights/reports/2017/african-american-women-our-science-her-magic.html

33. *Effie's Paper* – Amazing brand offering the best Black Girl Magic Swag. Please support fellow small businesses ran by minority women. ??
34. *All Hair Matters* - Black women upset about Shea Moistures #AllHairMatters, Amber Payne and Chandelis R. Duster, *Shea Moisture Ad Falls Flat Under Backlash*, NBC News, https://www.nbcnews.com/news/nbcblk/shea-moisture-ad-falls-flat-after-backlash-n750421
35. *Selling to Baby Boomers* - QuickSprout, *Forget Millennials. 7 Reasons Why Baby Boomers Are the Ideal Target Market*, https://www.quicksprout.com/marketing-to-baby-boomers/
36. *Emotional Selling* - Harvard Professor Says 95% of Purchasing Decisions Are Subconscious, Logan Chierotti, *Harvard Professor Says 95% of Purchasing Decisions Are Subconscious*, Inc., https://www.inc.com/logan-chierotti/harvard-professor-says-95-of-purchasing-decisions-are-subconscious.html
37. *How Customers Think* – Book by Gerald Zaltman, How Customers Think: Essential Insights into the Mind of the Market, Book, https://amzn.to/2K40FzV (Side note, I have not read this one)
38. *Millennials and Brands* - Stats on How Millennials Wish to Engage and Interact with Brands, Adobe/ Invoca Study, *Emotions Win: What Customers Expect in the Age of AI*, https://go.invoca.com/rs/769-GSC-394/images/What_Customers_Expect_In_The_Age_Of_AI.pdf

39. *REI* - Customer experience changes with data, National Retail Federation, *REI's Brad Brown on mapping customer journey,* https://www.youtube.com/watch?v=Z_YIppV8Svg

Improving Discovery with Search

45. *Jekyll Island Craziness* - G. Edward Griffin, *The Creature from Jekyll Island: Second Look at the Federal Reserve*, Book, https://amzn.to/2KPhnCR
46. *Schema Research* - Less than .3% are getting Schema Markup Correct, SearchMetrics, *Over a third of Google search results, incorporate Rich Snippets supported by Schema,* https://www.searchmetrics.com/news-and-events/schema-org-in-google-search-results/
47. *EAT* - Google's E.A.T Rating and General Guidelines, Google, https://static.googleusercontent.com/media/www.google.com/en//insidesearch/howsearchworks/assets/searchqualityevaluatorguidelines.pdf
48. *Google Algorithms* - Simplified Explanation of Google's Search Algorithms, Google, *How Search algorithms work,* https://www.google.com/search/howsearchworks/algorithms/
49. *Ad Blockers* - Greg Sterling, *Survey shows US ad-blocking usage is 40 percent on laptops, 15 percent on mobile*, MarketingLand, https://marketingland.com/survey-shows-us-ad-blocking-usage-40-percent-laptops-15-percent-mobile-216324
50. *Schema* - Example of Making Brand Connections
51. *Easy Creamy Herb Chicken* - Google Search Results

52. *Schema Results* - Google, Learn how content appears in Google Search, https://developers.google.com/search/docs/guides/search-features
53. *Schema Types* – Example of Different Schema Types
54. *Local Business* - Google, Structured Data for Local Business, https://developers.google.com/search/docs/data-types/local-business
55. *Product Images* - Google Structured Data for Product Image Search, https://developers.google.com/search/docs/data-types/product
56. *Reviews* - Google, Structured Data for Reviews and Ratings, https://developers.google.com/search/docs/data-types/review-snippet
57. *Events* - Google, Structured Data for Events, https://developers.google.com/search/docs/data-types/event
58. *Carousels* - Google, Structured Data for Carousels, https://developers.google.com/search/docs/guides/mark-up-listings
59. *Recipes* - Google, Structured Data for Recipes, https://developers.google.com/search/docs/data-types/recipe
60. *Top Places* - Google, Structured Data for Top Places List, https://developers.google.com/search/docs/data-types/top-places-list
61. *Videos* - Google, Structured Data for Videos, https://developers.google.com/search/docs/data-types/video

62. *FAQs Online Search*, Google, Structured Data for Videos, https://developers.google.com/search/docs/data-types/video
63. *FAQ Voice Search* - Google, Structured Data for FAQ Voice Assistant Search, https://developers.google.com/actions/content-actions/faq
64. *How To's* - Google, Structured Data for How to Actions, https://developers.google.com/search/docs/data-types/how-to
65. *Schema Resources* - https://Discoveredbook.com/
66. *Logos and Social* - Google, Structured Data for Logos and Social, https://developers.google.com/search/docs/data-types/logo
67. *Knowledge Panel* - Google, Wonder Woman, Knowledge Panels are SUPER DUPER powerful for online and voice search. AKA Knowledge Panel, Knowledge Graph, Knowledge Vault.
68. *Linked Open Data* - Live on LOD Live, http://en.lodlive.it/
69. *Kevin Bacon* - Mark Robinson, Movie Morsel: Six Degrees of Kevin Bacon, http://www.markrobinsonwrites.com/the-music-that-makes-me-dance/2018/3/11/movie-morsel-six-degrees-of-kevin-bacon
70. *LOD Cloud* - Linked Open Data Cloud from lod-cloud.net, https://lod-cloud.net/
71. *WordLift* - Check out WordLift's Solution to help with this process. To get 10% off, use this affiliate link https://wordlift.io/bethanienonami/
72. *WordLift Guide* - Read WordLift's Semantic SEO

Guide, wordlift.io/ download-semantic-seo-guide/

Assisted Search

75. *Path to Purchase* - The search journey is never linear, Google, How search enables people to create a unique path to purchase, https:/ / www.thinkwithgoogle.com/ feature/ path-to-purchase-search-behavior/

76. *Shopper Journeys* - Super cool interactive Shopper Journeys, Google, https:/ / www.thinkwithgoogle.com/ feature/ path-to-purchase-search-behavior/ journeys/ automobile/ car/ yuan

77. *Customer Experience Adobe* – CX Expectations, Adobe, *Helping businesses measure experience. Consumer experience expectations scores and insights.* https:/ / www.adobe.com/ insights/ measuring-customer-experience.html

78. *Visually Impaired* - Approximately 8 Million known blind people in the US, The National Federation of the Blind, *Blindness Statistics*, https:/ / www.nfb.org/ resources/ blindness-statistics

79. *Inside the Box* - A great book about complementary branding (co-branding), Greg A. Sausaman, *Inside the Box, The Power of Complementary Branding*, https:/ / amzn.to/ 2IiLbWw

Search Takeaways

80. *Simon Sinek* - Thoughts on Leadership's creation of a competitive environment, Simon Sinek, *Most leaders don't even know the game they are in -*

Simon Sinek at Live2Lead 2016,
https://www.youtube.com/watch?v=RyTQ5-SQYTo&t=658s

Voice Opportunity

84. *Voicebot* – Voicebot.ai Insider giving you the latest trusted voice industry data and trends. https://Voicebot.ai/Insider/
85. *Voice Assistant Timeline* - Bret Kinsella, Voicebot.ai, https://Voicebot.ai/voice-assistant-history-timeline/
86. *Voice Growth* - Rate is 121.3% compounded, Juniper Research, *The Digital Assistants of Tomorrow*, https://www.juniperresearch.com/document-library/white-papers/the-digital-assistants-of-tomorrow
87. *$45 Billion Voice* - Voice Commerce Estimate $45B, O&C Strategy Consultants, *Voice Shopping Set to Jump to $40 Billion By 2022, Rising From $2 Billion Today (2018),* https://www.prnewswire.com/news-releases/voice-shopping-set-to-jump-to-40-billion-by-2022-rising-from-2-billion-today-300605596.html
88. *3.25 Billion Voice Assistants* - Bret Kinsella, *Juniper Estimates 3.25 Billion Voice Assistants Are in Use Today, Google Has About 30% of Them,* Voicebot.ai, https://Voicebot.ai/2019/02/14/juniper-estimates-3-25-billion-voice-assistants-are-in-use-today-google-has-about-30-of-them/
89. *Juniper Paid Research* - To purchase Juniper's Full Research Report ($4044 USD, €3546, or £2990), Juniper Research, The Digital Assistants of Tomorrow, https://www.juniperresearch.com/researchstore/innovation-disruption/digital-voice-assistants
90. *Voice Adoption* - Activate Tech & Media Outlook

2018, Activate SlideShare, Activate Tech & Media Outlook 2018, https://www.slideshare.net/ActivateInc/activate-tech-media-outlook-2018/21?src=clipshare

91. *Voice Awareness* - Level of Consumer awareness of Voice, PwC, *Prepare for the Voice Revolution*, https://www.pwc.com/us/en/services/consulting/library/consumer-intelligence-series/voice-assistants.html

92. *Smart Speaker Voice Usage* - Voicebot.ai, *Adobe Says 91% of Business Decision Makers Investing in Voice Today and Voice Commerce is the Top Objective of 45%*, https://Voicebot.ai/2019/05/14/adobe-says-91-of-business-decision-makers-investing-in-voice-today-and-voice-commerce-is-the-top-objective-of-45/

93. *Smartphone Voice Usage* - PwC, *Prepare for the Voice Revolution*, https://www.pwc.com/us/en/services/consulting/library/consumer-intelligence-series/voice-assistants.html

94. *Prefer Voice* - over other behaviors, PwC, *Prepare for the Voice Revolution*, https://www.pwc.com/us/en/services/consulting/library/consumer-intelligence-series/voice-assistants.html

95. *Voice Assistants Control* - PwC, *Prepare for the Voice Revolution*, https://www.pwc.com/us/en/services/consulting/library/consumer-intelligence-series/voice-assistants.html

96. *KMart* - Gift Giving Voice Experience, Bret Kinsella, *Matt Ware and Lachlan Pottenger of First Talk Voice Shopping in Australia – Voicebot Podcast Ep 85*,

Voicebot.ai, https://Voicebot.ai/2019/02/25/matt-ware-and-lachlan-pottenger-of-first-talk-voice-shopping-in-australia-voicebot-podcast-ep-85/

97. *Oh Lord!* - 75,000 people asked the Church of England for help on Alexa, Christian Today, 75,000 people asked the Church of England for help on Alexa, data shows, https://www.christiantoday.com/article/75000-people-asked-the-church-of-england-for-help-on-alexa-data-shows/132530.htm

98. *Voice Takes Over!* - Digital voice assistants platform prediction, Ronan De Renesse, *Virtual digital assistants to overtake the world population by 2021*, Ovum, https://ovum.informa.com/resources/product-content/virtual-digital-assistants-to-overtake-world-population-by-2021

99. *Facebook AI* - Chief AI Scientist Statement about focusing on voice, Bret Kinsella, Facebook's Chief AI Scientist Says the Service Would Like to Offer Smart Digital Assistants. Here's Why, Voicebot.ai https://Voicebot.ai/2019/02/19/facebooks-chief-ai-scientist-says-the-service-would-like-to-offer-smart-digital-assistants-heres-why/

100. *Facebook Shareholders* – 2019 Meeting Statement about Voice, https://edge.media-server.com/m6/p/d5wo2w56

Voice Search

110. *Voice Search Prediction* - Voicebot.ai SEO Report, Voice Assistant SEO Report For Brands, Voicebot.ai https://Voicebot.ai/voice-assistant-seo-report-for-brands/

111. *Evaluation of Speech* - Google, https:// ai.googleblog.com/ 2017/ 12/ evaluation-of-speech-for-google.html
112. *Voice Results Vary* - Voicebot.ai SEO Report, Voice Assistant SEO Report For Brands, Voicebot.ai https:// Voicebot.ai/ voice-assistant-seo-report-for-brands/
113. *Trusting Strangers* - 84% people trust reviews online from complete strangers, Craig Bloem, *84 Percent of People Trust Online Reviews As Much As Friends. Here's How to Manage What They See*, Inc. https:// www.inc.com/ craig-bloem/ 84-percent-of-people-trust-online-reviews-as-much-.html
114. *Voice Answers Report* - Voice Search Answers Found, Rabbit and Pork (Agency in Europe), *Voice Search Ranking Report*, Roast, https:// wearerabbitandpork.com/ services/ voice-search-ranking-report/
115. *Voice Answers Image* - Voice Search Answers Found, Rabbit and Pork (Agency in Europe), Voice Search Ranking Report, Roast, https:// wearerabbitandpork.com/ services/ voice-search-ranking-report/
116. *Google Schema on Voice* - Accelerate your Schema & Voice effort with FAQ & How To's - Google Next Announcement, Google, *Enhance Your Search and Assistant Presence with Structured Data (Google I/ O'19)*, YouTube Video - 36 minutes, https:// www.youtube.com/ watch?v=GR1j2ADyGvA& feature=youtu.be&_ _s=mbjgisn2ikawsmhkeyb9
117. *No Answer Attempts* - Invoca, The Rise of Voice Report, https:// go.invoca.com/ ebook-lp-the-rise-of-voice.html
118. *Consumer Voice Questions* – Question Categories

on Smart Speakers, *U.S. Smart Speaker Consumer Adoption Report 2019*, Voicebot.ai, https://Voicebot.ai/smart-speaker-consumer-adoption-report-2019/

Voice Customer Experience

125. *Anti-Glass Slipper* - Dangerous Assumptions - Shoe Company Antonia Saint NY Kickstarter, Ashley Isaacs, The High-tech Heel & Flat Campaign That Took Kickstarter By Storm, Product Hype, https://blog.producthype.co/the-high-tech-heel-flat-campaign-that-took-kickstarter-by-storm/
126. *Voice Device Usage* - *U.S. Smart Speaker Consumer Adoption Report 2018*, Voicebot.ai, https://Voicebot.ai/voice-assistant-consumer-adoption-report-2018/
127. *Voice Activities* - What people are doing when they activate and engage with voice assistants, *U.S. Smart Speaker Consumer Adoption Report 2018*, Voicebot.ai, https://Voicebot.ai/voice-assistant-consumer-adoption-report-2018/
128. *PG Cruises* - Paul Gauguin Cruises, https://PGCruises.com
129. *Voice Assistant Usage on Smartphones* - 70% of smartphone owners have used their voice assistant in 2018. U.S. Smart Speaker Consumer Adoption Report 2019, Voicebot.ai, https://Voicebot.ai/smart-speaker-consumer-adoption-report-2019/
130. *Smart Speakers Battle Smartphones... Fight!* - *U.S. Smart Speaker Consumer Adoption Report 2018, Voicebot.ai, https://Voicebot.ai/voice-assistant-consumer-adoption-report-2018/*
131. *Smart Speaker Usage* - How shoppers are using

smart speaker voice assistants, *U.S. Smart Speaker Consumer Adoption Report 2019*, Voicebot.ai, https://Voicebot.ai/smart-speaker-consumer-adoption-report-2019/

132. *Shoppers Want in Store* - 62% shoppers want to go in store, *Voice Shopping Consumer Adoption Report*, Voicebot.ai, https://Voicebot.ai/voice-shopping-report-2018/

133. *Voice in Store* – 62% of Shoppers want an in-store voice shopping experience, Voice Shopping Consumer Adoption Report, Voicebot.ai, https://Voicebot.ai/voice-shopping-report-2018/

134. *Robocopy Conversational Academy* – Conversational Designer Course & Certification, https://conversationalacademy.com/courses/conversation-design-fundamentals?affcode=231963_29f5vako

Voice Commerce

140. *Amazon Shopping Triples* - Q4 2018, Robert Williams, *Alexa-powered shopping triples during holiday season*, Mobile Marketer, https://www.mobilemarketer.com/news/alexa-powered-shopping-triples-during-holiday-season/545063/

141. *Voice Commerce is Popular* - *U.S. Smart Speaker Consumer Adoption Report 2018*, Voicebot.ai, https://Voicebot.ai/voice-assistant-consumer-adoption-report-2018/

142. *What Consumers Buy* - Voice Shopping Consumer Adoption Report, Voicebot.ai, https://Voicebot.ai/voice-shopping-report-2018/

143. *Voice Shopping Orders* - Voice Shopping

Consumer Adoption Report, Voicebot.ai, https://Voicebot.ai/voice-shopping-report-2018/

144. *Voice Order Amount* - Voice Shopping Consumer Adoption Report, Voicebot.ai, https://Voicebot.ai/voice-shopping-report-2018/
145. *I like it a lot!* - What Consumers Like About Shopping on Voice, Voice Shopping Consumer Adoption Report, Voicebot.ai, https://Voicebot.ai/voice-shopping-report-2018/
146. *I don't like it* - What Consumers DO NOT Like About Shopping on Voice, Voice Shopping Consumer Adoption Report, Voicebot.ai, https://Voicebot.ai/voice-shopping-report-2018/
147. *Shopper Interaction* - How shopper wish to interact with brand ads, The Rise of Voice Report, https://go.invoca.com/ebook-lp-the-rise-of-voice.html
148. *Millennials AI* - 72% of Millennials believe that brands can use technology to predict what they will want to buy. Lucie Green, "Frontier(less) Retail," Slideshare Summary or Purchase the Full Report, https://www.jwtintelligence.com/2016/06/new-trend-report-frontierless-retail/
149. *Emotions Win* - Adobe & Invoca - Emotions Wins: What Customers Expect in the Age of AI, Adobe/Invoca Study, Emotions Win: What Customers Expect in the Age of AI, https://go.invoca.com/rs/769-GSC-394/images/What_Customers_Expect_In_The_Age_Of_AI.pdf
150. *Impact of AI* - Juniper Research, The Impact of AI for Digital Advertisers, Juniper Research, *The Impact of AI for Digital Advertisers*, Free whitepaper link https://www.juniperresearch.com/document-

library/ white-papers/ the-impact-of-ai-for-digital-advertisers You can order the full research here: https:/ / www.juniperresearch.com/ researchstore/ content-commerce/ ai-in-digital-advertising

Voice Use Cases

155. *Experience is Everything* – 1 in3 people walk away from a brand after a bad experience, PwC, Experience is everything: Here's how to get it right, https:/ / www.pwc.com/ us/ en/ advisory-services/ publications/ consumer-intelligence-series/ pwc-consumer-intelligence-series-customer-experience.pdf
156. *Positive Voice Experience* - PwC, Prepare for the Voice Revolution, https:/ / www.pwc.com/ us/ en/ services/ consulting/ library/ consumer-intelligence-series/ voice-assistants.html
157. *Lack of Voice Trust*- PwC, Prepare for the Voice Revolution, https:/ / www.pwc.com/ us/ en/ services/ consulting/ library/ consumer-intelligence-series/ voice-assistants.html
158. *Like About Voice Experiences* - Voicebot.ai, Smartphones Adoption Report 2019, https:/ / Voicebot.ai/ smart-speaker-consumer-adoption-report-2019/
159. *Quality Voice Experience* - Qualities people look for in a voice experience - Smart Speaker, Voicebot.ai, Voice Assistant Consumer Adoption Report 2018, https:/ / Voicebot.ai/ voice-assistant-consumer-adoption-report-2018/
160. *Why Use Voice More?* - Voicebot.ai, *Voice Assistant*

Consumer Adoption Report 2018, https://Voicebot.ai/voice-assistant-consumer-adoption-report-2018/

161. *Nike VUX* - Nike Google Action Skill, RAIN Agency, https://rain.agency/
162. *Voice Use Cases by Age* - Alexa Skills, https://AskMarvee.com
163. *Smart Speaker Demographics* - Ages that own smart speakers, Giselle Abramovich, *Study Finds Consumers Are Embracing Voice Services. Here's How*, CMO.com, Adobe, https://www.cmo.com/features/articles/2018/9/7/adobe-2018-consumer-voice-survey.html#gs.j1405c

Voice Strategy

170. *Top Voice Objectives* - for Businesses, Heidi Besik, *91% of Brands are Investing in Voice: How to Make it Work*, Adobe, https://theblog.adobe.com/91-of-brands-are-investing-in-voice-how-to-make-it-work/
171. *Sprint Book* - Sprint, *How to Solve Big Problems and Test New Ideas in Just Five Days* by Jake Knapp, Amazon, Print or Audible, https://amzn.to/31ppHyN
172. *Consumer Voice Reviews* - on Voice Platforms, Voicebot.ai - *Smart Speaker Consumer Adoption Report 2019*, https://Voicebot.ai/smart-speaker-consumer-adoption-report-2019/
173. *Voice Discovery* - How Smart Speak Owners Discover Voice Apps, Voicebot.ai - *Smart Speaker Consumer Adoption Report 2019*, https://Voicebot.ai/smart-speaker-consumer-adoption-report-2019/

174. *Voice Search Results* - in Actions by Google, Rabbit and Pork (Agency in Europe), Voice Search Ranking Report, Roast, https://wearerabbitandpork.com/services/voice-search-ranking-report/

175. *Product Inventory Feed* – Google Local Product Feed https://support.google.com/merchants/answer/3061198?hl=en

176. *Amazon's Choice* – Suggestions to increase your chances of becoming Amazon's Choice product. https://amzadvisers.com/get-amazons-choice-badge-products/

177. *Assistant Pro Rocks* - The company that does the stuff you don't want to do so you have more time to do what you love. Assistant Pro website, https://www.yourassistantpro.com/

Why Innovation Fails

190. *MIT Research Study* - Cliff W. Scott, *The Science and Fiction of Meetings*, MIT Research Study, https://www.researchgate.net/publication/265508855_The_Science_and_Fiction_of_Meetings

191. *Bill Gates* - Warren Buffet, and Charlie Rose Interview, YouTube Charlie Rose Interview with Warren Buffet and Bill Gates - YouTube Video - 52 minutes long https://www.youtube.com/watch?v=GF3sKyOSeYs

192. *How Sears Changed America* - Data about Sears, *How Sears Changed America*, CNN Money https://money.cnn.com/2017/03/23/news/companies/sears-changed-america/index.html

193. *Rise and Fall of Sears* - More data about Sears, Don

Davis, *The Rise and Fall of Sears,* the Internet Retailer, https://www.digitalcommerce360.com/2018/10/19/how-sears-failed-in-the-e-commerce-era-even-as-it-innovated-online/

194. *Amazon Innovation* - Greg Satell, *How Amazon Innovates*, Medium, https://medium.com/s/story/how-amazon-innovates-67747090c4d2
195. *Local Motors* - 3D printed car at Local Motors, https://localmotors.com/heritage/
196. *Quirky* - Company that help inventions get to market faster, https://quirky.com/
197. *Shall we play a game?* War Games Movie, https://www.imdb.com/title/tt0086567/

Innovating Customer Experiences

200. *Millennials Value Experience*- Christopher Donnelly and Renato Scaff, "Who Are the Millennial Shoppers? And What Do They Really Want?" Outlook: Accenture's Journal of High Performance Business, https://www.accenture.com/us-en/insight-outlook-who-are-millennial-shoppers-what-do-they-really-want-retail
201. *Sephora* - Retail "Phygital" (physical & digital experiences), Doug Stephens, Interview with Bridget Dolan, Reengineering Retail, 2017, Figure 1 Publishing
202. *Sonos* - Cool listening living room retail experience, https://www.sonos.com/en-us/home
203. *Globetrotters* - Outdoor adventure store, https://www.globetrotter.de/ - Open in Google Chrome so Google can translate the site for you.
204. *Pirch* - Shower and cook before you buy for your home, https://www.pirch.com/home

205. *Lowe's LoweBot* http://www.lowesinnovationlabs.com/lowebot
206. *Lowe's HoloLens* - VR home design experience, http://www.lowesinnovationlabs.com/project-visualization
207. *HoloLens Case Study* - Microsoft https://docs.microsoft.com/en-us/windows/mixed-reality/case-study-lessons-from-the-lowes-kitchen
208. *Customer Experience Index* - Forrester Summary of Report - https://www.medallia.com/resource/customer-experience-index-score/ Purchase the Full Report - https://www.forrester.com/report/the+business+impact+of+the+customer+experience+2014/-/E-RES113421#

Brand Innovations

209. *Retail as the Media* - Story Customer Experience - Story, Diane Hess, *Story founder touts 'community retail'*, https://www.crainsnewyork.com/asked-answered/story-founder-touts-community-retail

ABOUT THE AUTHOR

Bethanie Nonami is an inquisitive fixer, fast-driving, fun-seeking, food-lovin', lifelong learner, and self-proclaimed nerd on a mission to make this world a better place than when she first entered it. She also wants to put an end to all the miseducation circulating through cyberspace pertaining to search engine optimization. Whether it's through words, SEO, or marketing, she is up for the challenge. For nearly three decades, technology has been the focal point of Bethanie's life, and it all started during grade school (she was the first and only girl programmer in her fourth-grade class).

This thought leader is living proof that a conventional route to success isn't the only way to make an impact. In fact, she has an impressive track record of working tirelessly in order to succeed while helping others do the same. At the ripe age of 22, she was the 1st Sales Engineer at a global fortune 100 company hired without a degree. Even before that, she was all about the hustle, working late shifts at Domino's and drag racing cars during high school. Now, she not only has a debut book out, she serves as a Chief Innovation Officer at Marley Nonami. You can reach Bethanie at Bethanie@DiscoveredBook.com or on LinkedIn.

www.ingramcontent.com/pod-product-compliance
Lightning Source LLC
Chambersburg PA
CBHW070938050326
40689CB00014B/3251
9780578541648